SNIFFING
the
CORK

SNIFFING

the

CORK

AND OTHER
WINE MYTHS
DEMYSTIFIED

JUDY
BEARDSALL

with C.B. deSwaan

ATRIA BOOKS

NEW YORK LONDON TORONTO SYDNEY SINGAPORE

ATRIA BOOKS
1230 Avenue of the Americas
New York, NY 10020

ISBN: 0-7434-3800-0

First Atria Books hardcover printing July 2002

10 9 8 7 6 5 4 3 2 1

ATRIA BOOKS is a trademark of Simon & Schuster, Inc.

For information regarding special discounts for bulk purchases,
please contact Simon & Schuster Special Sales at 1-800-456-6798
or business@simonandschuster.com

Designed by Jaime Putorti

Printed in the U.S.A.

ACKNOWLEDGMENTS

❖

Thank you to everyone who made this book possible, including writer Connie deSwaan, one of the bravest and most professional people I have ever been fortunate to work with.

Thank you to Al Lowman, my agent, who believed so passionately in this project.

My thanks to my editor, Mitchell Ivers, whose enthusiasm has been a delightful asset throughout this creative process.

CONTENTS

Introduction: Of Goddesses and Grapes   *ix*

1: Wine Sense   *1*

2: The Grand Wine Tour   *25*

3: Wine, Health, and Beauty   *59*

4: A Walk through a Wine Shop   *83*

5: Between Shop and Table   *101*

6: Wine for Special Occasions   *117*

7: The Restaurant Experience   *137*

8: Collecting Wine, Wine Accessories,
and Antiques   *173*

Bibliography and Resource Directory   *197*

Index   *201*

Herein, Misobibists, expect a shock . . .
(Not) does it only for the flesh provide,
For grace and beauty in the glass reside.
The long-stored sun and sweetness of the South
Enrich the mind as warmly as the mouth.

—Sir A. P. Herbert
   An excerpt of his poem, from the foreword
   to his *Kinloch's Wine,* 1961

INTRODUCTION:

OF GODDESSES
AND GRAPES

———— ❖ ————

I've always been in love with wine.

Inspired by the words of the master of interpreting myths, Joseph Campbell, who said, "Follow your bliss," I have managed to seamlessly unite my work in the wine trade with my passion for it. I consider that not only blissful, but a great blessing. This book is my way of sharing this passion with you.

When I went into the wine business twenty-one years ago and decided to make it my life's work, everyone said, "Judy, it's a boy's club—it'll be difficult to break into." The wine business was a very daring career choice for a woman to have made in 1981. I didn't know where this interest in wine would lead me. Nor was I given much encouragement.

I literally begged for my first job at Sherry-Lehmann, the most upscale wine shop in New York. From that point, I used to worry, where could I go? I had no career model to follow and there was no postgraduate degree to pursue. So I carved out a career in the wine trade by myself, little by little, not knowing how it would evolve. I just knew what I loved and that was enough.

Ultimately, I worked in every aspect of the wine trade—buying, selling, investing in, transporting, storing (including designing and building custom wine cellars), preserving, and presenting wines of every style, value, and from every point of origin.

Perhaps Ambrosia—a Roman bacchante, or follower of Dionysus, the wine god—was one of the forces guiding me on my career quest. Ambrosia, after all, was turned into a vine. On a more earthly plane, I was also inspired by Nancy Drew, the ever tenacious, curious, and fearless girl detective. If Ambrosia inspired the passion, then Nancy knew how to pursue the truth and get her plans into action. Thus, I figured out how to solve the "mystery of the wine trade," listening with half an ear to warnings that I could never have a future in this very narrow world—while nevertheless steadily learning and succeeding in the business. The more the mystery, the more the challenge, the more the warnings that I would fail, and the more my determination to continue on.

Today, I've reached a place I thought I could never realize—making my own wine from a wonderful vineyard in Italy. I have named the wine Cinnamasta, inspired by another great and powerful earth goddess. In following my bliss, it has also become my mission to make wine pleasurable and rewarding for others.

Wine is my passion—and I hope that as you read this book, it will also become yours. Wine is meant to be drunk, not just sipped, and I am happy to see more people opening a good bottle at home, even if it's on hamburger night! And although some French farmers might disagree with me on this point, the only meal at which I would *not* include wine is breakfast.

This book is meant to address the many issues people have put to me over the years. I've heard what concerns or confuses most nonexperts about the wine experience. In *Sniffing the Cork,* I can finally answer the questions I'm most frequently asked, and the questions I *should* have been asked more frequently, about wine.

It is also a wine book that *pointedly understands and includes women.* Times have changed, but a waiter or a sommelier still rarely hands the wine list to a woman at a restaurant if she's with a man. However, it *is* almost always presented to the man at the table. The reason is clear: Women still aren't expected to know a whole lot about wine, before or after the bottle has been opened, while men, historically, *are* presumed to know about these things. This is the first wine myth I am determined to change!

For women, wine has always been a food—one of the many flavors, sensations, and experiences that make life better. Wine enhances their table and their hospitality. Little by little, men's attitudes are changing. In the last several years, men have begun to treat wine as less of an accessory or a status symbol—like a Cuban cigar or a high-ticket sports car—and more as a natural element of the pleasures of the table.

Wine is one of the most ancient gifts of the gods and goddesses and one of humankind's greatest mysteries. Pleasure giving and health enhancing, wine has been honored and described in ancient texts, including the Bible. Wine has the capacity to be both an everyday and a celebratory drink. Including wine in your life every day is good for both body and soul. Western European countries have a heritage of an inclusive wine culture that goes back centuries. In those areas of America where vineyards are part of the landscape, such as

California, Oregon, and even parts of Long Island in New York State, wine is a natural element of daily life. It can even be, as you'll discover later in chapter 8, a real and viable investment.

I came upon the word, "misobibist," which was coined in the early part of the last century by a great wine lover, Sir A. P. Herbert, and used in the poem that opens this book. Misobibists are people who hate drinking wine. Ironically, I liked discovering this word, which encapsulates a certain ongoing antiwine sentiment—which, for me, is so sad. Wine is, after all, life enhancing and here to be loved.

So, most of all, I hope this book encourages you to search out wines that fit your tastes. Get to know your local wine shop. Try to include wine in your life no matter where you live in this country—and share my life's passion.

And may *Sniffing the Cork* inspire you to follow *your* bliss. *Salute.*

SNIFFING
the
CORK

1

WINE SENSE

❖

I recently had dinner with a friend who wants to know enough about wine to bottle it. Literally. It's no secret that Tom would like nothing more than to toss his day job in advertising and start his own vineyard. I have big hopes for him.

We were at a neighborhood Italian restaurant on this occasion and we ordered a decent bottle of Barolo. Dinner conversation with Tom always leads away from chatting about the fate of friends or current events to talking about our mutual passion: wine. More to the point, we talk about our *philosophies* of wine. That night Tom said something that struck me as a perfect summary of what wine can be.

"For me," he said, "I look at the passion, the intention, and the style behind the wine."

"For me," I added, "I seek a true sensory experience."

We knew exactly what we each meant.

People are always stunned when I talk about wine in these terms. You'll rarely catch me rhapsodizing in the kind of standard or arcane wine jargon that doesn't tell anything about the experience you have *in the wine*. I look for ways to describe the passion, the intent, the style, and the feeling of wine. When I talk with people who make wine, I understand their dedication and knowledge of the land. When sensory feeling meets the passion, intent, and style in a glass of wine, it can transform you.

Wine is a sacrament of the earth, and the vines were here long before human beings stood upright and beat down paths to find grapes growing wild. Grapes are farm products, and growing vines is a combination of agricultural skill and knowledge of the local natural characteristics of the soil in which they're grown. That grapes have an astonishing and delicious changeability when they're made into wine is one of those eternal mysteries. Thousands of years ago, someone figured out how to tame and improve the growing of grapes and learned how to turn them into the wonderful liquid you find in your glass.

When you open a bottle of wine and the fragrance wafts up, you're smelling the fruit of the earth, just as when you walk through a field after it's rained and you feel a joy in that fantastic, fresh, wet grass. That's the heart of what's happening in a glass of wine, too—a coming back to the earth, a connection with nature.

I'm a very practical woman, but with wine, I believe in this theme and want to pass it on to you: *Understand the earth first, then the glass!* This is where your wine experience begins.

UNDERSTANDING THE EARTH

Local soil character makes a difference, and you taste this difference in the wine. For example, people always ask me: "Why is Champagne from France supposed to be better than sparkling wine from California or Australia?" Champagne comes from Champagne country in France—a real region that has a unique combination of chalky earth, a specific climate, and exposure, unlike anywhere else.

The grapes that become Champagne from the Champagne region in France have a particular magic. You can't recreate them quite exactly the same, even if you were to get cuttings from the best vines and plant them in a place called "New Champagne." You can't import those other X factors and manufacture the same wine anywhere wine is made in America or in Australia or elsewhere. You can't make *that* Champagne happen in a laboratory either, no matter how much money you poured into the project. Therefore, real Champagne has a taste that is distinctively *from* Champagne.

The French have a catchall term for these X factor qualities: *terroir,* which refers to that elusive congruence of a particular soil with a particular place in a particular climate.

Someone who owns a vineyard on one side of the hill with a southwestern exposure and a certain kind of drainage and gravel subsoil will make a completely different kind of pinot noir than the grower whose patch of land on the other side of the hill has a northwest-facing slope with a slightly different subsoil. This is *terroir.* What is produced in this elusive foundation of elements is nature in action.

Like Champagne, each wine-making region of the world produces wine with a fantastic character of its own and can give you a sense of place. Heights of brilliance can be reached in wine making—and a few lows get in there, too. Some wines are so magnificent that they can't be replicated. Other wines are so poor or barely mediocre in quality that they shouldn't be replicated. But good or bad, wine connects to you immediately with a sense of place. Until your palate is trained to know the effect of *terroir* on the difference in taste and character between wines, the label on the bottle will give you information and a place to start learning.

I remember a trip to a village in the Dolomite Mountains, situated in the very rocky terrain on the border of Austria and Italy. They make fantastic white wines—and also good reds—up in those mountains. Eating the native food and drinking the local wine, I believed the world was in harmony. No one I dined with analyzed the acidity of the particular Gewürztraminer we were drinking. They just know that Siegfried down the road made this wine and that it was a fabulous accompaniment to the cheese, made by Anna on the other side of the mountain.

This wine had a character it wouldn't have anywhere else, a character just like the people who lived there. A resident of the Austrian Alps has certain qualities that are different from someone raised in, say, southern France. The same is true for distinctive differences in the wines that are produced in various wine-making regions around the world. The qualities that make us—and wines—different are what is so wonderful about nature.

Unfortunately, there's an international style of wine making that's becoming popular. Some wine makers are producing wines that have the same flavor profile as their competitors' products and are stylistically indistinguishable from them. It's rather like looking around and seeing how eight out of ten people are pretty much wearing the same clothes. This homogeneity makes it more difficult to find wines with true personality, individuality, and a sense of where they came from.

Wine is a very personal food. I admire the small wine makers everywhere. When wine becomes an industrial product, that thousands of bottles a day assembly-line stuff with no character, you lose the gift of the handmade wine and the dedication that went into it.

So I hope this book will help you walk past the mass-produced wines and do yourself a favor: *Try wines by smaller vineyards, whether from California, Spain, New Zealand, or anywhere else.* The shock is that you can get a really terrific bottle of wine for the same price as the wine that's bottled as if it were soda pop! Wine with character, style, passion, and personality doesn't have to be expensive. You can always get something really distinctive without breaking the bank.

Before you learn the differences between wines, there are the key elements in appreciating wine itself. Here is the most important starting point: wine standards.

WHAT'S GOOD AND WHAT'S NOT GOOD?

I have a lot of opinions about wine, but I've studied the industry and know there are standards in wine that go beyond personal choices and tastes. As much as I like to debunk myths, I believe in certain standards that equalize and maintain wine quality. These standards can help you draw lines between good and bad, great and sublime.

The wine business has standards that may differ from region to region and country to country, but all serious wine growers strictly adhere to quality control. You cannot simply buy a parcel of land and say you're going to make wine without first knowing the industry and government standards of your area. In some regions, you can't use certain chemicals and, in other areas, specific growing practices are followed.

There are very strict rules and reasons for every standard of wine making—which is one reason why some wines are better than others. These standards also mean a better drinking experience.

I consider the importance of standards in another way, too. I often worry that people think about names too much: *They don't drink the wine, they drink the label.* Let's declare an end to this counterproductive snobbery.

I did a fun wine tasting for a client in Connecticut who invited forty people over for the occasion. I set up four reds and four whites and kept one of the whites covered up to play the role of the "mystery wine." The tasting was not about what you *knew* about wine but *what you liked.* There was one common thread: All the whites were made from the same grape, but they were all different and ranging in retail prices from $18 to $80 a bottle.

Everyone walked around the table and sampled each of the wines. I provided them all with a list of the wines they would be tasting, so they knew the names of three of the four whites. The big question was, "Which wine do you like the best?" A simple show of hands went unanimously for that $18 bottle of wine—the winner over the "mystery" bottle which, it turned out, was the one that sold for $80.

The trick I played on them was that the mystery wine really was a fabulous bottle, but way too young to drink and not yet revealing its full glory. It would be wonderful in a few years, but those with a sophisticated palate would have picked it out. The whole idea was, *are you drinking the label or are you drinking the wine?*

Only three or four people voted for the mystery wine as the favorite. When I finally told them what it was, a man yelled, "Oh, you're kidding! You got me! That's my favorite wine. If I'd known what it was, I would have voted for it!" For the rest of the evening he would come up to me and say, "You got me! How could you do that?" I told him as diplomatically as possible, "You didn't vote for it because you didn't see the label." His attitude is really not about appreciating the wine so much as applauding a good label. He was not a wine drinker, but still an unconverted label drinker.

Again, the issue is appropriate standards: Although they were all made from the same type of grape, that $18 bottle had as much integrity as did the $80 bottle. You shortchange the wine and your experience of it if you say, "If I'd known which was the more expensive bottle, I'd have chosen it over the cheaper wine." Two different wines must be measured by two standards of quality.

Let me make an analogy: A violinist playing a Stradivarius violin is going to produce a better sound than a violinist playing on a fiddle from Violins 'N' Things. However, you're not expecting the fiddle from Violins 'N' Things to sound like the Stradivarius. The grapes that were grown to make that $18 bottle of wine came from a piece of land that is not rated as having the potential to make a wine as glorious and symphonically exciting as the wine that comes from that vineyard where the $80 bottle of Corton-Charlemagne was made.

A bottle of Corton-Charlemagne is expensive because it is *expected* to perform. There's a history to this wine as well as the astonishing pleasure that can be derived from sipping the ultimate.

When you're devoted to having a good experience in that glass of wine, something stirs and happens in you. You understand the concept of having standards, and learning a bit about them will only enhance your enjoyment of all kinds of interesting wines.

UNDERSTANDING WINESPEAK

I once clipped out a full-page ad for Bordeaux wines paid for by the Bordeaux Wine Information Bureau. The ad is an alluring picture of a wineglass in gradations of red shades with the word "Bordeaux" superimposed on the glass. The glass was set on red velvet, with candlelight and hints of lip-staining kisses in the background. It's terribly French, creating allusions to lovemaking and the alluring connection between wine and love.

Nowhere do they use words like "plummy" or "tobacco-y" to suggest the taste or aroma of the wine they're tantalizing you with. Instead, they've successfully illustrated the *feelings* this wine evokes: sensuality, intimacy, warmth, and pleasure. Not bad for a glass of wine.

People have tried diligently to put into words what wine does to you, as depicted on that page. So, in a way, if I asked you to describe what a kiss tastes like, you wouldn't really qualify it with a "like" statement. *You'd connect it to a feeling.*

We've gotten accustomed to hearing wine experts/columnists/critics use words to describe a specific wine as tasting or smelling like, say, "candied fruit," "tropical flowers," or "gooseberries in autumn." Sometimes they write that wine is "flinty" or "green." Other times the description can be totally baffling, as when they describe wine as "structured" or "complex."

A wine merchant I know of described one of his white wines as "smelling like Sophia Loren after a brisk jog," a funny and provocative association. A perspiring and iconic Italian movie star definitely provides an image that suggests a pleasurable interlude with the wine, if not the star herself. The great British guru of wine, Michael Broadbent, also loves to use female allusions in his published tasting notes. He wrote about a 1959 Château Latour that it was "like Jane Russell—mean, moody and magnificent."

These subjective descriptions often make more sense to me than typically arcane winespeak. A newspaper wine columnist recently described a Chianti as reminding him of "red brick" even though, of course, he most likely never tasted brick. This kind of analogy stumps me. It asks you to imagine how red brick smells and tastes before you can imagine what the reviewer savors in a good Chianti.

This is not how I like to think about it. I want to know how the Chianti makes me, or you, feel. What sensual associations click with the taste and aroma. Then, if it helps, we can describe the sensation in winespeak. Or not.

Last summer, I was with a client who loves wines, but to her credit, she is not a person who uses typical wine language to describe what she's drinking. She'll either like the wine or not. Then she'll try to make an effort to learn its background and history. Susie's not overanalytical, either; she's immediately able to connect to the pleasure of it, which is a great way to be.

I brought over a bottle of Italian wine for Susie to taste

and was a little nervous. This bottle was very different from the French wines I knew she preferred. It was wine from Piedmont in Italy, made of the Nebbiolo grape, and like some French Burgundies, is extremely subtle. You have to focus on it a bit more when drinking it. I was in the dining room at her house decanting it when she walked in. I offered her a taste and said, "See if you like this."

Susie took a sip, and I stood there, swirling my glass, concerned that she didn't say anything for a while. I gave her some background on the area by saying it was the part of Italy that's famous for truffles and game. The wine is a delicate, but paradoxically powerful wine. So she sipped it and then she looked at me, still silent. I thought, "What can I do if she doesn't like it?" When she smelled it again she said, "Oh, Judy, it's wonderful. It's like looking through a veil."

I thought, isn't she fantastic. I was very happy. Susie connected brilliantly with the feeling of the wine by using her senses—without having to intellectualize and use a wine vocabulary. She came up with an analogy that she'll always remember. *I'll* always remember it too. I was moved because it said everything. It was one of those perfect moments that wine lovers treasure.

DEVELOPING YOUR OWN WINE LANGUAGE

The vocabulary to describe wine was really developed for the purpose of like-minded professional buyers, tasters, and people on the professional side of the business. These terms help in symposiums or tastings or professional situations in which wines are being evaluated and the professionals need a common terminology. Winespeak facilitates the process of business and standards. The problem is that when winespeak filtered down to the public, it inadvertently became an accessory people felt was de rigueur for their enjoyment of wine.

This is a myth.

While I'd like to change the unsaid rule that classic winespeak is the *only* way to communicate wine feelings, I also know that it's impossible *not* to use some of the accepted wine terminology. If I use these terms, it's because they're clarifying at the moment and appropriate for the occasion. But my real arguments with classic winespeak are that it's limited and emotionless.

Winespeak should *not* define your experience—and this is my real point: You don't have to sound like an expert to love the drink in your hand. You don't need to know if wine is "robust" or has "surprising acidity" or any other descriptive words before you can enjoy it.

I have a favorite little book by cartoonist Ronald Searle in which he talks about "the tortuous phrases that are frequently used" by some wine critics and reviewers. Searle praises a few of them as "remarkable poets, those whose words vividly conjure up unimagined nuances and have us panting to experience the excitement and glow of drinking a particular bottle." But he says that wine writers like that are as rare as the greatest vintages. Then he talks about the other, not so remarkable, not so poetic folks, who may have all too much influence on the choices we make. He calls them a "grotesque international band of snobbish, inarticulate" people "incapable of thinking beyond their insular little circles" who "do as much harm to the world of wine as they do to the language." He hopes for their silence with the sarcastic, "Their day will come."

While Searle is tough on these reviewers and critics, I admit to a love-hate relationship with them. I know they want others to love wine the way *they* love wine. My problem with them is that their language doesn't in the end inspire as many people as they think it does.

I picked up a little English book called *Wine-Tasters' Logic* which addresses this thorny subject, too. The author, Pat Simon, throws fuel on the winespeak wildfire. He says, at the risk of being politically incorrect, that certain wines are still classified by gender—thought of as masculine or feminine. Château Latour, for example, is considered a masculine, broad-shouldered, big wine. The distinctive perfume of a great Château Margaux, on the other hand, is considered very feminine. Such gender descriptions may or may not help you get to the feeling of a wine.

I prefer to think of a really good glass of wine as like a very well played piece of music. Music and wine both have harmony, balance, and style. Every vintage plays a different interpretation of the grape. A good glass of wine, like a great piece of music, changes your vibrations. They both affect you physically, emotionally, and intellectually. Throughout the ages, poets and songwriters have sung the praises of wine because it is about tonality and melody in a glass. Add in color and fragrance and only then does it all meet language.

Whether it's the smell of jam, a roast chicken, cooking peaches, or herbs, we spend a lot of time talking about what wine is "like." Why? Our entire sensory systems build up pattern recognition. We can still read text even if half the letters are smudged or truncated. We can figure out who's in a solarized or profile portrait if portions of that person are recognizable to us. We can immediately identify a song from a mere tease of the melody.

These are truly wonderful expressions of the heights of cognitive evolution to which we have come. This is partly why we look for analogies: Our cerebellums were conditioned to associate one thing with another—probably as a survival tactic. We can identify aromas that are familiar to us, even sense memories back to when we were babies.

Do we have to say that the wine smells like violets or flint or even bricks? Would a description like, "a rich outer layer and a vibrating core of red fruit inside" or "intense with lots of vibrant Sangiovese fruit" really help you understand the taste experience? Probably not for most people.

Some terms that are widely accepted by experts are not meaningful to most of us. Wine reviewers may talk about a wine as being "steely." Have they ever tasted a piece of steel? I have put a piece of stainless steel in my mouth in the form of an eating utensil. Forks and spoons taste metallic to me, which is different from "steely." The other common term, "flinty," is another word associated with munitions that I can't associate with the deliciousness in my glass.

Throughout my career, I've perused charts that are meant to help people understand wine by its flavor, I assume, to simplify matters. There are flavors that are associated with white and red wine. White wine flavors, for example, may have the flavor attributes of grass, pears, lemons, or apricots. Red wine may have aspects of berries, chocolate, or currants. Some wine experts suggest you sip wine and identify these flavor attributes.

I like to say, "I want the wine to speak to me, I don't want to speak about the wine." Develop your own wine vocabulary. If wine smells like clean sheets or peeled apples to you, then express it without fear. Appreciate wine and the feelings it gives you. It's not about naming the flavor or the fragrance.

Having said that, we can't just say there's no such thing as words to describe wines. There *are* words.

Let's not worry about the language of wine. Here are my suggestions for learning about it:

- You really have no way of understanding the wine-speak until you taste the wine. Then, maybe, you can make the same association, but it doesn't matter if you do or not!

- If you never learn to put any words on the taste of wine, all you really have to do is enjoy the experience.

- The sensory associations you make with wine are your own and are as valid as any expert's.

- The more you taste wines from good-quality vineyards from all over the world, the more easily you will learn to distinguish between taste and aroma—and the more you learn about wine in general.

WINE AND STYLE

When my friend Tom talks about wine having style, I know exactly what he means. I sometimes like to use fashion comparisons to make my point about a wine. You may not know anything about wine, but you can immediately identify with fashion and style.

If you see a gorgeous outfit in a magazine, you understand the feeling it gives you. You also appreciate the difference between a designer outfit and a similarly styled outfit made by a mass-market manufacturer. The quality of materials and the cut determine the cost and which one you'll buy. Both designs are valid and can bestow upon the wearer the feeling of being stylish, whether the outfit comes from Givenchy or the Gap.

So a Beaujolais, for example, would be like a pair of jeans—a casual classic, always young in spirit. Jeans have their place, too. You wouldn't wear them to a dinner party or black-tie wedding. Likewise, you'd be more likely to enjoy that Beaujolais at a picnic or barbecue, rather than at a black-tie event.

Other wines can be compared to other fashion classics: A wine can be like a suit by Armani or a dress by Versace. The first is elegant, subtle, and structured; the second is a bit daring, wild, and colorful. Both descriptions capture the designers' flair—and both descriptions can capture the intent of certain wines.

Part of style is balance. With fashion and clothing, balance

THE MYTH
OF
CORK SNIFFING

One of my pet peeves is *cork sniffing*, which is nothing more than a theatrical flourish!

The importance of cork sniffing to determine the quality of the wine is one of those oft-repeated wine myths, which, like most tales, spring from an arcane bit of truth. Sniffing the cork tells you nothing about the wine.

Only the most knowledgeable and highly trained specialists in the field of oenology can detect a possible taint on the cork—the effect of a cork mold—which could potentially affect a wine's taste, and then only sometimes. This is not a skill anyone other than such a wine expert can genuinely perform.

So, discounting the rare experts, if you're at a restaurant and the waiter or the server smells the cork, you're witnessing affectation in action. If you're at a dinner party, and your host sniffs the cork, the verdict is the same: It's a bit of pretension that should have been avoided. And if your host or the server smells the cork and actually makes a remark about how splendid the aroma is, you know better!

---

is achieved by proportion and fabric choice. In music, balance is attained when the orchestra or band members and/or the vocalists come together and create a symphony of harmonious sound. You feel that confluence immediately. With wine, balance includes: fruit, alcohol level, and acidity, all of which impart the flavors, textures, and impressions of a great sensory experience in a glass of wine.

THE SENSORY COMPONENTS OF WINE

Since the wine experience begins for me with appearance or color, let me start there.

COLOR OF WINE

Wine is a feast for the eyes even before you take the first taste. Most of us aren't conditioned to stop and look at wine, but it's the start of the fun. Pour a glass and take a moment to notice and admire the color.

Most wine bottles are green, so you can't see the true wine color. There's a good reason to put red wine in green bottles: simply to protect it from the light. I don't think you'll ever see a bottle of red wine that's not in green glass. But the myriad variations of reds or whites stress the argument for only pouring wine into clear glasses, or if you choose to, into a clear glass decanter.

Describing wine colors is a bit like looking at fabric swatches, with astonishing variations of whites; yellows; purples; and reds in different opacities, tranparencies, and textures. There are thousands of variations and depths of color related to wine. Reds can be a deep red, as opaque and dark as a mahogany stain. There are rich, lush reds and the deep purple of a young wine. Some wines are so opaque, you can't see through them to the bottom of the glass. Others are light and clear.

How Best to See the Color of Wine

Once you've got at least a third of a glass of wine, *don't* hold it up to the light or at arm's distance in front of you. Instead, take your glass and tilt it slightly against a white surface or napkin. You'll see the *real* color. Shades of color extend from the middle of the glass to the rim when you tilt it, too.

White wines vary in color, too, although the visual experience is totally different from that with reds. With whites, you look for depth, clarity, and shadings of color. Some white wines are nearly colorless while others are a deep honey amber; others are greenish in hue. Some whites are gold straw yellow, lemon yellow, or green tinged. Other white wines turn a pale gold or golden with age, depending on the wines and whether they are dry or sweet. White wines can even get coppery in color and are gorgeous to look at.

Color can tell you a lot about the maturity or condition of a wine. If it's browned out, the wine could have been badly stored or it may be mature but past drinkability. White wine can fade, showing gradations of color. Fading—meaning the color pales out toward the edges—has a bad connotation and usually implies that the wine has lost its intensity.

Young healthy red wines, as a general rule, show a very

deep purple or mulberry purple before they begin to mature. A common term people use for this stage of maturity is "ruby colored." As they age, many but not all red wines take on different hues, sometimes invoking words like "garnet" (like the semiprecious gem) or "warm orange" at the rim. These are the subtleties, but if a red wine is very yellow or brown at the rim, it's probably past its peak. However, some wines that are aged can have a very tawny or amber tone, which is different from brown or yellow at the rim, and can be quite delicious.

THE SMELL OF WINE

Color is glorious, but not as pivotal in appreciating wine as is smell. The human sensory capacity for distinguishing smells amounts to about ten thousand different scents. Seems impossible, but it's true.

Like flavor charts, aroma wheels are staples in many wine books. They are usually big charts with categories like black-and-red fruit, herbs, spices, flowers, and all the possibilities that wine can smell like. If you were seeking, for example, an intense black currant-y aroma, you'd be directed to a Cabernet Sauvignon.

If you want to identify the difference between black currant, blackberry, plum, black cherry, strawberry, raspberry, red currant, red cherry, it's definitely a delicious and fascinating pastime. I do it myself because it's part of my passion for wine. I love to say, "I really *do* smell currants in this wine."

But there are some scents in wine I don't know and *you* won't know. I didn't smell an actual, fresh gooseberry until I was nearly thirty years old. Gooseberries aren't as common a berry in America as they are in Scandinavia or England. Yet there are wines consistently described as having the aroma of ripe gooseberries, so I was out of luck in this department for years. I was always disappointed.

Down to basics: About 90 percent of *taste* is *smell,* which I think is the stepchild of our senses, so aroma is a big part of drinking wine. We respond consciously and subconsciously to our sense of smell all day long—we're animals who are in tune with our environment and the people around us. If you smelled the smoke, you'd know there was a fire and run from the house. With wine, you need to tune in to a more subtle scenting skill.

Even if you never learn to name the scents in a glass of wine, you already know many of them. Take a rose. A woman who walks into the room wearing tea-rose perfume fills the room with an identifiable, if manufactured, scent. Most people presented with a fresh rose immediately put the flower to their noses. But they rarely make a leap of association to say, "The smell of a rose is like my grandmother's back yard on a summer day when I was three years old." They either think it has a beautiful scent or, if they don't like roses, a noxious fragrance.

Wine and its connection to the sense of smell can open up an intoxicating new world for you, but it takes practice and a bit of focus. It's not unlike wanting to play the piano better. You take lessons and need to practice. Makes sense. If you want to really put that nose in the glass and smell some of the scents that are associated with wine, you'll need to begin sense memory training. Start by smelling, for example, pears and figs and honey and butterscotch. Then open up a bottle of wine and pour yourself a glass.

What Does Tannin Mean?

If, in your travels, you encounter a wine that makes your mouth feel like you're puckering up, blame the tannin, or tannic acid, in the grapes. This puckered feeling is the same when you drink a cup of tea in which you left the tea bag in for too long a time.

Tannin has that astringent quality, signaling that you're probably tasting a very young wine that's not ready to drink.

Some experts say that tannin helps red wine to age but this is a very general statement. It's a variable in the big complex world of age worthiness and greatness in wine.

The Taste of Wine

Taste is actually a less refined sense than the sense of smell. We think we're tasting without the sensory boost of smell, but that's not so. If you hold your nose, either you won't taste anything or you'll mute the flavor drastically. We talk about taste because most wine language describing wine comes from its nose, or "bouquet," which is really how it smells.

More than any other drink, wine is capable of an amazing variety of flavors and styles. Is it crisp, medium dry, fairly light, slightly astringent, or sweet, for starters?

I was at a dinner party recently when a woman across the table asked me, "What do you do when you're in a restaurant and the wine you ordered tastes too acidic? Can you send it back?" What she meant, she told me, was that the wine tasted "vinegary" to her and she didn't know if her bad experience meant the wine really was, or probably wasn't, good.

If a wine doesn't taste good, it may *not* be good, but then again, it may not be to your liking, and there's nothing wrong with it at all. This was a difficult question in the extreme, since I hadn't tasted what she tasted while she was eating dinner.

What I know is true is this: What tastes good to you is sometimes simply a matter of *familiarity* with a specific wine. This familiarity can breed an acquired taste. Curiously, many of the most notable flavors are not immediately likable. "Acquiring a taste" is a common enough occurrence with foods like caviar or escargots or a fermented drink like beer. Certain foods or drinks may be culturally alien to you, in which case you need to make a positive effort to try them. Fish eggs, garlicky snails, or a malty brew may not hold gustatory magic for you the first time out. There are some wines that you'll love immediately, while, as with caviar, other wines will be an acquired taste.

For example, in my travels, I've found that Chardonnay is conventionally, if not nearly universally likable. This is not true for Sauvignon Blanc—Sauvignon deriving from the French word *sauvage,* meaning wild. This wine is less easily likable on first impression, but like caviar, Sauvignon Blanc has a singular taste that ultimately wins you over.

What's it like? I'd rather tell you that Sauvignon Blanc is a grape that grows nicely in many places all over the world and give you a list, ranging from France to New Zealand.

THE "FINISH"

Finish is about the *aftertaste.* One of the marks of great wine is how long the flavors last. Finish is sometimes called "length." They're similar but have different characteristics.

The French have a word for finish, which is *caudalie,* actually the name for the flash of a second flavor that you taste after you've swallowed the wine. Finish is also a measure of the length of flavor, so you might sip a wine and say, "This wine has great finish."

I'd rather add that Sauvignon Blanc is a grape that makes a fabulous array of white wines. But I will say that, mostly, you'll adore Sauvignon Blanc, which can taste tart and lemony or round and very "gulpable."

"Mouth Feel" of Wine

What makes more sense than wine having a mouth *feel?* Or, simply, how does it feel in your mouth? This is a really fascinating quality to contemplate.

Mouth feel involves the matter of *body.* It's not just the alcohol, but also the sugars and the esters that give wine its dimension. This part is very sensual. Take a sip of wine and ask yourself, how does this wine feel? Watery? Smooth? Is the mouth feel heavy or beefy, like a person who's too pumped up? Does it make your mouth pucker up or feel sticky? Is it velvety? These sensations are pretty easy to identify.

Mouth feel is a sensation in the same way that running your hand over a piece of cloth describes feel. You know by the surface if it's wool or polyester, scratchy or smooth, silky

---

"Legs"

In the business world, "legs" mean your product has staying power and can run into the future. In the wine world, legs are the telltale signs of a wine's viscosity that show up on the glass.

So what *are* legs and what do you look for? To determine the legs of a red wine, swirl a small amount of the wine around in the glass, then hold the glass upright. You'll see little streams running down the inside of the glass that briefly cling to the sides. These are the legs. Generally all wines will have them.

I don't usually look for legs in the wine I drink, but people who *know* wine tend to talk about the subject.

---

or nappy, lightweight or heavyweight. You should be able to evaluate the mouth feel using the concept of texture. Is it tingly on your tongue? Is it *frizzante?* as the Italians would say.

THE SOUND OF WINE

Sound is the least involved of our senses in terms of appreciating wine, but three sounds stand out: the squeaking of a cork before it pops out of a bottle, the dull pop when it comes out, and the sound of wine being poured into the glass.

There is nothing I don't like about wine drinking, unless it's bad wine.

SNIFFING THE GLASS

If sniffing the cork is pretentious, what about sniffing an emptied glass to figure out what wine you've been drinking? This was a first for me and I saw it happen on my flight back from Rome:

A man sitting across the aisle called the steward over to order another bottle of the white wine he'd been drinking. However, the steward had taken the bottle, and the man didn't notice whether he'd been given Pinot Bianco or Chardonnay. So, how do you order "another" bottle of a mystery wine?

Without hesitating a fraction of a second, the steward took the man's glass—with a few drops of wine in it—dipped his nose in delicately and sniffed. "Pinot Bianco," he said.

Only a continental wine lover could so unselfconsciously sniff another man's wine glass!

2

THE GRAND WINE TOUR

❖

An old acquaintance called me one morning and said, "My sister gave me a fantastic bottle of Margaux for my birthday." I thought, a Margaux? How lucky. Then she added, "I'll tell you the name of the wine." Aha! Something entirely different.

"It's called Rausan-Segla," Anne read from the label. Hers was a wine from the *Margaux region* in Bordeaux, not a bottle of *Château Margaux,* a whole other story in great wine making. "I want to have a fantastic dinner to go with this wine and you're invited. What should I make?" she added eagerly.

The vintage of the wine was a 1996 and it was then 1999. "When do you plan on making this dinner?" I asked. "Your wine is still too young to drink. If you open that bottle, you'll get a lot of mouth-drying tannin and less pleasure out of it. Give it another six or seven years!" Instead, I recommended a fantastic bottle of wine that would be worthy to drink in the next week or so.

Anne's inadvertent confusion about the value and pedigree of her bottle of wine (Château Margaux, the property) with the *region* (Margaux) in which it was made turns out to be a cousin of a common misunderstanding about wines. The more typical mix-up, especially in America, goes like this:

If you've ever been in a wine shop and asked for a bottle of Chardonnay or Chianti or Burgundy or Beaujolais, you have a preconceived notion about what you're buying. If there is any confusion about wine, it's at this most rudimentary level: the *grape/region* dilemma, or mistaking the kind of grape that makes the wine for the area of a wine-making country whence it comes.

The facts are: Merlot is a grape and Bordeaux is a region in France. Chardonnay is a grape and Burgundy is a region in France. Gamay is a grape and Beaujolais is a region in France. Riesling is a grape that grows in Germany and elsewhere and Champagne is a region in France. Sangiovese is a grape and Chianti is a region in Italy, and also the name of a wine.

If you're confused, it's because sometime in the 1950s, a few California wine makers decided to market their products under the generic type of grape or a famous wine-making region in Europe. This explains why lots of Americans believe that Burgundy is always a red wine. Not true; there are delicious white Burgundies. Such labeling may definitely sell wine, but calling the wine Burgundy or Merlot doesn't mean that it's necessarily good. Either one could be lousy, or depending on the producer and where the producer's vineyards are, it could be the most expensive wine in the world.

To add to the confusion, European wine producers have

their own national and local rules for labeling wine and usually name their wines for the region of production rather than
the grape. Let's take a popular wine like Chardonnay.

The designation on its own tells you very little because
Chardonnay is the name of a *grape* that grows all over the
world. It's one of the most versatile, adaptable vines growing
in the hot climates and various soils of South Africa,
Australia, and California (some of their best wines are made
from Chardonnay)—in fact, in many regions in the world. In
each region where it is made into wine, you get slightly different flavors and different character—yet Chardonnay re-
tains characteristics that are immutable. It has rich aromas
and a fragrance that you can learn to identify.

The popularity of Chardonnay in America is a relatively
recent phenomenon, because twenty-five years ago there was
very little of it grown outside of its hometown in France.
There, the Chardonnay grape is made into many, many different wines, the best of which come from a region called
Burgundy. It has the best soil, the best climate, and the mysterious X factor that make Burgundian wines a subject of intense scrutiny.

Ultimately, Chardonnay has become a tag line to simplify
white wine buying. But if the label says Chardonnay, then it's
going to be from anywhere else in the world but France. The
French do not call wine from their Chardonnay grapes
Chardonnay, but they use the Chardonnay grape to make
everything from Chablis to Puligny-Montrachet to Pouilly-
Fuissé to Mâcon-Villages to Champagne.

Whatever the wine from whatever grape or region, what's
really important is the human element in the wine-making
process. This begins with the people who grow the grapes and
make the wine. Wine is a very personal food. I admire the

small wine makers everywhere. When wine becomes an industrial product, that assembly-line stuff with no character, you lose the gift of the handmade wine and the dedication that went into it.

VINTAGE

The word "vintage" as applied to wine simply designates the year the grapes were harvested. It does not automatically imply rarity or that a vintage wine will routinely be more expensive.

However, if you check the label on a bottle before you buy it and there is *no* vintage, drop it back into the bin and move on. That eliminates every jug wine you can think of. In a nutshell, the year a wine is made is important and can tell you a lot about how good or not good the wine may be. Harvests vary tremendously from year to year all over the world.

Every year the weather is different, even if the soil is the same. Weather affects the grapes and there's no two ways about it. Drought does one thing to them. Frost another. If it pours rain for too long, you've got a "wipeout" during the harvest. That's what it can feel like to a vintner—being on a surfboard and getting hit by a wave and going over. In this case, the grapes swell with water, like placing a berry in a glass and putting it outside in a storm. Not only does it get waterlogged, but when you taste it, the flavor is diluted.

Every harvest counts. Even in difficult years, some of the usually great wines from great producers may not be marketed as *great*, but *good enough*. Wine makers may sometimes produce a vintage and then sell it off to supermarkets.

Vintage is one of the most important details in choosing

good wine. There's no way to guess about it, so you have to taste a wine or get a recommendation from an expert who knows something about vintages in various wine-growing regions. Of course, every year in every region there's a different story.

But if it doesn't have a year, don't buy it, except for Champagne, where nonvintage is always good.

WINE BASICS

Wine may have an alcoholic content, but it's not a distilled spirit, like vodka or blended scotch. Wine is an organic product, and no matter how processed it is, you can't knock all "the natural" out of it.

I was reading a little book by a favorite writer on wines, Jancis Robinson. She discusses a little of the natural chemistry of wine, which people tend to ask me about all the time—for example, the difference between light and full-bodied wines and the range of alcohol content.

Robinson makes a comparison I can't argue with, which is that, just like people, wines have a weight. A wine's weight is a measure of how much extract and alcohol it has. It may not be as easy to discern light from heavy wines simply by looking at them in a glass. You'll need to note the alcohol content on their labels, then smell and taste them. Some red-wine comparisons, for example, are easy: A red Bordeaux has a depth of color that, say, a Beaujolais does not.

If you like the details, fermented grapes usually have between 12 and 14 percent alcohol. Every bottle of wine is required by law to have the alcohol percentage on the label. The number can be written in degrees like "13.5 degrees," or as a percentage, as in "13.5 percent."

Full-bodied wines can have an alcohol content of 14 percent. Lighter wines contain less than 10 percent alcohol, often about 8.5 percent, which Jancis Robinson calls a "much flimsier specimen." I agree.

GIVING WHITE WINE ITS DUE

I love red wine and tend to prefer it over white, except when it comes to Champagne. Reds get the respect first and are thought of as the premier important wines while whites suffer a bit from neglect.

I may love reds, but the good whites don't disappoint me. I want both my children to be loved equally by others. "White wine is a fall-back drink," a client told me unceremoniously when I recommended a white wine, a wonderful Riesling. "Tell me about a great red instead."

> ### THE ART OF WINE
>
> "The alcohol in wine is as the canvas upon which an artist paints a picture. . . . It is not the small percentage of alcohol that appeals to you, but the brilliant ruby of the wine's color, the attractive perfume of its bouquet and the delicious savor of its farewell, the lingering taste which it leaves behind as it descends smoothly down your grateful throat."
>
> —André Simon

"Let me tell you about a great Riesling," I responded. "You'll change your mind about white wines." I told her that Riesling is made from a beautiful, noble, and outstanding grape. I had a Riesling in mind for her from Germany. (The grape name is often part of German wine labeling along with the village name or vineyard name.) I told her that this white wine is rich, complex, and delicious and that she shouldn't turn down a chance to try it.

White wine is *not* a back-up drink when nothing else is around. It is not the bottled spring water of wines, or a chilled, mildly flavored default drink. It's not a lesser red or a wanna-be red that pales by comparison. It's not a wine-flavored wet wonder, but the real stuff. White wine can be totally wonderful and should have character to it, aroma, taste, and memorable flavor.

Let's go around the world with wines and start in France with the whites.

FRENCH WHITES

The former president of France, Charles de Gaulle, once asked rhetorically, "How can you govern a country which produces 246 different kinds of cheese?" He was said to have captured the French character in that statement.

For me, the French are the kings of the vineyards. Never mind 246 kinds of cheese, what about 13,000 plus wine producers alone in *one* fertile southwestern area called Bordeaux?

The first thing that comes to my mind about France is that it's a relatively tiny place compared to America or Australia, other wine powerhouses, with very distinct wine regions. There are so many areas of France that produce wines, from dry to sweet, red and white varieties, from simple table wine to collectible masterpieces that you need a few lifetimes to sample all of them.

We begin in Bordeaux with its unique *terroir,* the combination of soil, weather, the slope of a hill, and altitude that grows terrific grapes. You'll get the real plums of the wine world from this region. There's a range of wonderful wines made at *châteaux,* or wine estates—in fact sixty-one legendary red wines from classified growths are made here at historic estates, or as they are known in Bordeaux, *crus* or *grands crus.*

While there's lot of snob appeal in buying one bottle or cellaring a few cases of the superstars like Château Lafite or Château Mouton, you can get great buys in Bordeaux wines among a different classification called *cru bourgeois.* These can be as good as some lesser qual-

> ### WHAT IS TERROIR?
>
> In the way that *terroir* generally translates to meaning place, the word *cru* simply means growth, but so much more. The French love wine as much as their debatably descriptive concepts about it.

ity classified *crus.* You can buy these wines for very reasonable prices in the $15–25 range.

Across the country from Bordeaux and its great estates you'll find Burgundy, the other legendary wine-making region. Located in eastern France, Burgundy is known for really fine red and white wines with great full flavor and for two chief grape varieties: Pinot Noir (a red Burgundy) and the familiar Chardonnay (from which white Burgundy is made).

This is where the French can confuse us. Weighty books have been written about Burgundy, its bounty, and its laws governing production.

What you need to know about Burgundy is that it is the most complicated region in the whole world to understand because the quality of the wine you drink depends so much on the person who makes it. After that, you need to know the vintage (second in importance) and then the name of the vineyard producing it.

There are at least eight hundred different wines made here, each named for the village it comes from. Then the villages are subclassified, and there are many villages and subsections of the village. Then there are different *crus* within each village. Wine producers can operate on patches of land that extend from half a hectare to twenty hectares, which means every vineyard is relatively small. A vineyard can have one owner or fifty or more owners. Ultimately, each wine is made somewhat differently.

However, when it's white wine, it is made from only one grape and no other: the Chardonnay grape. When you drink a white Burgundy, you're drinking the Chardonnay grape. Chardonnay wines are made in other regions, but they are not great white Burgundies. Thank the *terroir* and the loving hands that tend it.

If you love white Burgundy, you can validly complain that there's never enough produced each year. Try to get your bottle. For good value look for a bottle of simple "Bourgogne Blanc" on the label. The wine will be balanced, delicious, and a really good value, especially when it's from certain producers such as Leroy or Domaine Leflaive.

Moving around France, we go southwest to the Languedoc, which is producing more and more fantastic wines, mostly reds. The Loire Valley region, which stretches across the northwest of France, produces a lot of nice red and white wines with its cooler climate. The Chardonnay grape doesn't thrive here, but instead white wines are made from the lively Sauvignon Blanc and red from the Cabernet Franc. The two principle white wines from the Loire Valley are Sancerre and Pouilly-Fumé, known to be the slightly more full-bodied of them. Don't confuse Pouilly-Fumé, a Sauvignon Blanc-based wine, with Pouilly-Fuissé, which is made from the Chardonnay grape in Burgundy.

Loire Valley wines are friendly and delicious and most of them don't need much age. You just buy them and drink them. They shouldn't be expensive at all.

Since we're in northern France, let's stop at Alsace in northeastern France. Its location and its name tend to confuse people, who mistakenly place this region across the Rhine River and into Germany. The history of Alsace has been as one of those border territories disputed over and tossed back and forth between nations. It officially became part of France after World War I and its wines have a French sensibility with a German twist.

Alsace wines suffer a little from an image crisis because tradition put them into those skinny long-neck bottles that people associate with German wine. We see such a bottle and think, "A sweet German wine in a '50s style bottle—not for me." I urge you to look beyond the packaging: Alsace wines, dry or sweet, are terrific and can be some of the best bargains around.

Alsace wines (please, not "Alsatian"—an Alsatian is a dog) are some of my favorites, ever. One of the best producers in Alsace is an old family business called Domaine Weinbach, run by a woman and her three daughters. It's one of the best white wine producers in the world, and their names are on the label of their wines: Domaine Weinbach (Collette Faller et Ses Filles).

These women are famous in the wine world and they make both incredibly expensive and really affordable wines. They work sixty-two acres of some of the best vineyards in one of the hills in a certain valley in Alsace. Each vineyard spot has a different designation of quality. Try them all. All the small vineyards in Alsace bring an individual character to the wines they make.

Recommendation: Alsace wines from the producer Zind-Humbrecht.

When I buy a bottle of wine from Alsace, I know I'll have a delicious experience, whether it's from a little-known or small producer with a good reputation or a big producer like Hugel or Trimbach, who make a lot of good-value wine.

Our final stop in the white wine *tour de France* is in Champagne—the name of a wine and the name of a place and the only place in the world where real Champagne is made. Sparkling wine is made all over the world. Champagne is about an hour's ride east of Paris and a fabulous day in the country. Instead of taking a coffee break, take a Champagne break. This wine is really good for you, body and soul.

Truman Capote thought so too. When he was asked to describe Cristal Champagne, he wrote that it was "a chilled fire of such prickly dryness that swallowed seems not to have been swallowed at all, but instead to have been turned to vapors on the tongue and burned there to one sweet ash."

Capote spoke about Cristal in a way that was distinctive, vivid, and meant something to him. "One sweet ash" on your tongue is a mighty incendiary thought about a sip of Champagne. Over the top? This is how wine can move you. It's emotional above the technical. Open a bottle of Cristal and then tell me if it's so.

Officially, Champagne is only Champagne if it is made in this region of France, otherwise it's really sparkling wine. There's no such thing as California Champagne, even if it's made from grapes growing on a vine transplanted from the source.

Champagne's got its own *terroir,* a chalky soil being just one component, and Champagne makers have their own trademark touches in producing it. There are different kinds of Champagne, which depends on the grape. Blanc de Blancs, for example, is made from all Chardonnay grapes, but most Champagne is a blend of mainly Pinot Noir grapes. These blends are unique to each "house," which is what Champagne companies are called.

Of all the wines, Champagne is the one that's most associated with joy, milestones, upward shifts in fortune, and a sense of luxury, if only momentary, while hoisting the glass. Champagne is elegant hedonism (very French) but so is it glamorous, and being practical again, an all-purpose wine. It's also the drink of consolation and the drink that goes with any food, even a burger. Drink it in a fluted glass, not the flat saucer glasses, so you can enjoy the bubbles, the aroma, and the taste better.

As for chilling the wine, I've had a glass of Dom Perignon Champagne at room temperature and it was delicious, full, and tasty. When it's too ice cold you don't taste it as much.

From this, I developed a formula: If the wine is great, drink it room temperature to coolish. If it's mediocre, or worse, the colder it should be.

A few last

The First Champagne

Champagne was originally a still red wine without bubbles. An accidental or unintentional second fermentation in the bottle caused the bubbles, which were the beginning of what we know as Champagne. Its discovery is attributed to the monk, Dom Perignon, who is claimed to have said, "Look, I'm drinking the stars."

words on French Champagne: Each of the three hundred or
so houses making Champagne, whatever its name, may produce magic in the bottle or not. Not all Champagne is wonderful. There are huge Champagne producers who crank out
millions of bottles of nonvintage Champagne. There are
smaller houses, who make wonderful bubbly, like Pol-Roger.
I like their wine style, which is very Yves St. Laurent—original, colorful, elegant. Bollinger is another good house which
makes Champagne in a range of prices. But if you see the
word "Champagne" on a French label, the wine probably isn't
going to be bad.

Should you buy vintage Champagne? Vintage is not nec-
essary to the true Champagne experience. Nonvintage
champagne, a blend of several different years, is also very
good.

If you want a nice sparkling wine from France that's not
Champagne and that's inexpensive, the oldest sparkling wine
in France is called Blanquette de Limoux, made near the
Pyrenees. Or try a sparkling Vouvray from the Loire Valley.
These wines are very light and not overly exciting, but have
their own integrity.

By the way, Champagne will never run out of grapes, no
matter what rumors tell you different.

FRENCH REDS

My love affair with red wine started in France.

For red wines, the place to go to first is Bordeaux and
then back to Burgundy. There are also great reds in the very
important Rhône Valley and the huge southwestern region
known as the Languedoc. Bordeaux, being the most illustri-

ous, is the home of good wines and the most impressive wines—the crème de la crème, the collectors' items. If you're serious about red wine, Burgundy and Bordeaux are wine heaven, so think about beginning your research here!

Let's begin in Bordeaux.

The dominant grapes here are Cabernet Sauvignon and Merlot, with some other types used in most blends. The wines from Bordeaux are named for the châteaux, the vineyards, and the properties that make them—some properties are vast and famous while others are small and obscure.

When you go to a wine shop, you wouldn't ask for a Cabernet Sauvignon if you want a Bordeaux. They're two different kinds of wine. In Bordeaux, wines are usually made of blends and rarely 100 percent of one grape, say, Merlot grapes, or another, such as Cabernet Franc. Merlot imparts a soft flavor while Cabernet Franc lends "structure."

Let's talk flavor. A wine label that says "Bordeaux" has, when it's very, very good, a complex blend of aromas and flavors. There are aromas you can easily detect which enhance your experience—some people liken the aromas to black cur-

---

"Mr. Merlot"

Our friend, the Merlot grape, has become the Pouilly-Fuissé of the early twenty-first century. Both captured a wave of popularity, turning them into almost generic wine types, making for ease of ordering them in a restaurant.

Calling a wine "Pouilly-Fuissé" (a wine named for a region and made of Chardonnay grapes) or "Merlot" caught on as a marketing trick. The French normally would *not* use the word "Merlot" on their bottles. However, some producers have started to mimic the American trend, so you will see the word on some bottles of French Merlot.

rants or plums. Some say chocolate or coffee beans. You can smell something reminiscent of cedar or even the emanations from a cigar box when you open it up. These are the classic, centerfold flavors in a good Bordeaux.

Again, we're talking *terroir*, so one vineyard contiguous to another may grow the same grapes but make completely different wines. This is how it goes: In Bordeaux, wines will be rarified and whatever is made is going to cost you. But it's worth the freight.

Vintages really are important in Bordeaux, because wine making is not about human intervention, but as I've emphasized throughout, it's about soil and climate. Great wines are made in the vineyard.

A good Bordeaux needs a couple of years of age. Whatever Bordeaux you buy off the shelf, you should give it time to age. Some of these wines mature more quickly than others, for example, the '97s, in which you might find good values as well as in the '99s. The '91s and '92s weren't great. Those years Bordeaux had too much rain, which diluted the flavor of the grapes.

Then there is the Rhône region in the southeast of France—of which there are two parts. You really have to talk about north and south as distinct wine-making regions. In the north, you'll find the exotic Syrah grape, while in the more southern climes of the Rhône Valley, Grenache is the grape variety of choice.

Syrah is a tough little fruit and easy to like. It's characterized by a very gutsy, spicy, peppery, kind of seductive flavor and has a rich purpley black color. I guess the most familiar flavor it brings to mind is blackberries, but with a fresh grinding of earthy black pepper. It's a grape that thrives in a hot climate.

The Rhône Valley Syrahs are herbal and smokey, and the good news is you can probably find them easily enough. Since this is the Rhône area, you'll probably find the wines blended a little bit where Syrah predominates. In the south, they definitely do more blending of Syrah with Grenache. The Grenache is a heat-loving grape with a softer, rounder kind of flavor, tempering the spicy Syrah. All these wines have one characteristic in common: that spicy, warm-climate taste. You can find a good Syrah for about $10.

You may have heard of Châteauneuf-du-Pape, a favorite Rhône red blended from Grenache, Syrah, and a few other grape types. This wine is usually good because the people who make it have a lot of integrity. And as to *terroir,* chances are the sun shines kindly down here. If it's not a great year for them, it'll probably be a *good* year.

You can also find good simple wines such as Côtes-du-Rhône in a wide range.

In the Languedoc region in southwestern France, you'll also find nice wines made from Syrah and many other grapes. Here, wineries will sometimes, but not always, name their wine for the varietal rather than the property or area.

Let's go to Burgundy and the exceptional Pinot Noir grape. It is the only grape grown in Burgundy that makes great red wine and is the most complex grape of all. Pinot Noir is the prima donna grape, fragile, capricious, and difficult to grow and make into wine. France, of course, is the benchmark for Pinot Noir-based wines that are called red Burgundies.

This is the wine that makes wine obsessives even more obsessive. A great red Burgundy is a holy grail pursued by wine lovers and wine fanatics everywhere. When a bottle of this wine is great, it is greater than anything in the world and it's *very* expensive.

The tiny pieces of land owned by lots and lots of different people make a myriad of brand names that can be very confusing. The world of Burgundy is fascinating, which is extraordinary since if you look at a map of France, this area is about as big as the head of a pin.

Sometimes I feel that opening a bottle of Burgundy is like inviting to dinner a temperamental opera star who's just had a tour canceled. Do you want to take a chance? If you're really sure of yourself and your other guests, yes. And if you really know opera, yes. Then you might have that tenor to dinner, but you know what? If you don't know anything about the opera world or what this singer has gone through to get where he is, you will really not be doing anyone a favor.

The same is true with Burgundy on your table. This is a wine for people who want to spend the money and still take the chance. There's nothing I love more than a bottle of *great,* aged red Burgundy. What can happen in that bottle in a great cellar in a great vintage from a great producer is haunting! More amazing, you get to drink a bottle that's been put down perhaps fifty years ago. Somehow that bottle got here, miraculously coddled, and fabulous. But maybe not.

Let me stress this point: Burgundy wants coddling (just like that tenor). Talk about not traveling well. These wines, like people, can suffer jet lag but they may never recover from it. The same bottle from a producer's cellar in France will be a different wine by the time it gets to America, not because any changes are made to the bottle in any way, but because it is temperamental.

I'm conflicted about this, so, no, I don't suggest you send out for the stuff. Instead, if you want to drink a delicious bottle of red Burgundy, call Air France and fly to the town of Lyon—smack in the heart of Pinot Noir country. Drink it in a nice bistro there and have an authentic Burgundy experience.

Next on our tour, Beaujolais is a region in Burgundy known for its eponymous red wine, probably one of the most familiar in the world. To drink a really good Beaujolais you don't need kid gloves. Quite the opposite. Beaujolais is best drunk young.

Only one grape is used in making Beaujolais, and that is Gamay. Gamay taste is much more forward, easy to enjoy and has a nice perfume to it. In flavor, it ranges from the simple, to the quite beautiful and full bodied, to the complex and layered.

DRINK THE GOOD STUFF

Beaujolais needn't cost a lot, but I urge you not to buy the cheaper mass-produced stuff. Unfortunately, this lesser Beaujolais gives me a headache and will probably give you one, too. Avoid cheap Beaujolais.

❖

There are ten specific villages in Beaujolais that produce the higher quality Beaujolais wines known as *cru Beaujolais*. These *crus* have more depth and not only take a little aging, but can improve with age. The people who make them have a lot of style and the *crus* have lovely names like Fleurie, Moulin-à-Vent, and Saint-Amour. Then you get something really interesting, not expensive and you're drinking Burgundy.

ITALY

Italian wine is my new passion. If there is one place in the world that is inspiring the most wine excitement these days, it has to be Italy. With superb variety and quality emerging

from every region of this country, there is an inexhaustible
amount of wine to taste and learn about. When you apply the
Italian creative sensibility to the pleasures of the table, you
have a winning combination for the good life—as more and
more people are finding out.

Italy produces lots and lots of wonderful red wines. Today,
Italy's white wines are coming along in quality and there are
many fine ex-
amples to be
found. Like the
French, or more
so, every Italian
has wine with a
meal. Life with-
out wine would
be desolation. A
friend of mine

> ### Which Wine, When?
>
> I have a good rule of thumb. The less expen-
> sive the wines, the more ready they are to
> drink, although some of them benefit from
> some time in the bottle. The more expensive
> wines have a structure to them that needs
> time to develop in the bottle. You'll taste the
> difference.

in Italy hired a married couple to farm, work, and live at his
wine estate. After a few weeks, he noticed that they seemed
very depressed. Concerned, he inquired if they were feeling
all right.

The wife replied, "Oh, yes, except we are not used to
drinking coffee for breakfast, and that is what you give us. We
are used to having wine with breakfast."

The situation was immediately remedied and the couple
happily worked there for the next forty years.

Italy may be the biggest wine-producing country in the
world with some of the most luscious and distinctly Italian
wines made from native grapes, like Nebbiolo, Barbera, and
Sangiovese. While France has it regions, Italy has its zones
where the wine business is concentrated on growing one or
two types of grapes to make many different kinds of wines.

The Nebbiolo goes into making Barolo, a potentially great red wine, while Chianti is a blend of Sangiovese and other grapes.

Italian Whites

Some of my favorite wines of all come from the Piedmont (on the northwest) and the Alto Adige (in the northeast). Italy shines with reds and if you seek their whites, go armed with information. A few large companies have made a popular success of marketing Pinot Grigio, but to me it tastes like mass-produced stuff. Pinot Grigio from small producers is better.

With Italian wines, you want to look to the more sophisticated market in the Alto Adige, or as it is also called, the Südtirol. They have more of that cool, mountainous northern climate. They're using different varieties, similar to Pinot Gris. They're making Chardonnay, they're making Sauvignon Blanc, they're using all those same grapes, but they're making them in Italy, and so they have a distinctively different style.

Climbing in the Dolomite Mountains, you might be tempted to break into a few verses of "Edelweiss." I love this area of the world, I love the wines, and I love the people. Many of the really good wines here are getting more distribution in the United States. You should be able to find more of them now.

I've saved a label from a Pinot Bianco, which I ordered while having dinner at the Oyster Bar in Grand Central Station. The wine was absolutely wonderful. The label is designed in such an old-fashioned way, it could have been made in Germany a hundred years ago, and it probably was. I didn't expect such decorative artwork on the label when I ordered the wine, I just picked its name off the list.

The wine was made in the Alto Adige region, which borders in part on Austria. It had one of the longest names I've ever seen, combining both German and Italian, and was a 1998 vintage from a region whose wines never once failed me.

My clues were the following: I wanted a white wine and I knew the Alto Adige was the place on the wine list to choose from. I didn't know the vintner, but I know that the people in that part of the world really are small producers dedicated to perfection and handcrafting their wines, simple or not. In a wine shop, it might cost about $12.

When you walk into your wine shop and head down the aisle toward Italian wines, you'll probably find a multitudinous array of choices. But if Italy has said *arrivederci* to anything, it's to that clichéd, basket-covered Chianti bottle that once represented Italian wine making. These emblems of friendly table wines are still around—supermarkets in Italy have shelves and shelves of them for sale—but the quality of Chianti, along with so many other Italian wines, has dramatically improved.

Generally speaking, when I think of Italian food, I think of red wine. Italian whites are really coming into their own as well, and there's no excuse now to drink an inferior bottle of Pinot Grigio at an inflated price.

Travel south of Rome toward Naples to Campania where, for example, wine makers are producing some delicious whites from all sorts of local grape varietals. One producer to look for is Feudi di San Gregorio, which has a range of whites that are perfect for before dinner or to drink with light fish dishes. On a recent wine discovery and tasting trip in Italy I tried some very tasty wines from obscure grapes like Vermentino and Ansonica. In the hands of scrupulous small producers and under advice from top oenology consultants, these will be *the* wines of the future for delicious whites at a reasonable price for quality.

Italy is an astonishing place and there are so many regions to explore: Tuscany, Piedmont, Lombardy, Friuli, Trentino-Alto Adige, Lazio, Sicily, and more. My personal cellar has grown from a primarily French one to include more and more Italian wine. Also, Italian growers and producers are also now working with varietals usually associated with French vineyards, such as Cabernet Sauvignon, Merlot, Syrah, Chardonnay—and they're drawing new dimensions on the international wine map with their modern styled wines.

A whole new breed of what are called SuperTuscans with evocative names like Sassacaia, Solaia, and Testamatta stand among dozens of other wines being sought after by serious wine lovers and collectors worldwide. These new kids on the block have become a force within the last twenty years. The most illustrious types of Italian red wines such as Brunello di Montalcino (made primarily from the Sangiovese grape), Barolo, and Barbaresco (these last two made from the subtle power of the Nebbiolo grape) can come from many different producers and are highly recommended.

Vintages do matter: The 1990s saw an unprecedented string of good-to-great vintages depending on the region. The years 2000 and 2001 are also very fine vintages.

We've been looking to the Italians for marvelous fashion, and now they are performing in the world of wine. Brava!

The Dom Perignon of Italy

Bellavista gets my vote when I'm looking for a very elegant sparkling wine from Italy. It's made in the same way as French Champagne, but this one comes from Italy's Franciacorta region, in the northwest of the country.

Bellavista is worth seeking out. Just don't call it Champagne— call it Franciacorta!

SPAIN

Spain's wine bounty holds a special place for me, since my first foray into thoughtful and serious wine purchasing started with Rioja, a renowned wine region in the north-central part of the country. Before I ever thought about a career in wine, I was attracted to these red wines, some best drunk young, some best aged. I read somewhere that Riojas are "strawberry and cream scented." It might sound to you like we're talking about confections, but actually, this is an easily recognizable way of approaching some of the aromas of these wines.

Back when I bought my first bottles of Rioja, they were good and they were affordable. The quality is still there, but they are no longer the bargain they were in 1980. Right now, they compete in both quality and price with the best of all their neighbors. Try a Rioja from a good producer. Ask your wine shop for a suggestion.

Spain makes another wonderful wine that tends, mistakenly, to be considered so far out of fashion that it's as dated as a wrist corsage. It's called Sherry, and no, you don't have to be over sixty to love it. Sherry is made in sun-baked southwestern Andalucia where the Spanish produce a range of Sherries from dry fino to the beautiful sweet Sherries called Oloroso. There is a dry Sherry called Manzanilla, which I love. It is made closer to the seacoast than other dry Sherries and is said to convey the scent of the sea air.

Spanish red wines originate from a number of interesting regions. Other than wines from Rioja, look for Penedes, Ribero del Duero, and Priorato. One of the world's most expensive and collected wines comes from Spain—Vega Sicilia—with a luxury-goods price tag.

GERMANY

When you talk about Germany you're talking about white wine that ranges from very dry and light to very rich and sweet. The quality can be forgettable or it can create one of the greatest wine experiences in the world. We are not talking about the mass-produced stuff, for which Germany's reputation as a fine wine-producing country suffered for a long time.

Germany makes fantastic sweet wines, which they're famous for, but all German wines aren't sweet. *This is a myth.* Some German wine makers sent over mediocre wine in the 1950s, '60s, and into the '70s. You had to be a connoisseur to really know how to find a great German wine.

The German wine business is very complex and the marketing people haven't made it easy for American wine drinkers who are not fluent in German to understand the labels. Very complicated laws in Germany regulate the labeling of wine, which includes the village name, the vineyard name, the producer name, the type of grape, and the

A Few More Words on Describing the Taste of Wine

Wine tasters tend to look for similarities to other flavors and scents they know or can imagine. I once read that Michael Broadbent, a wine writer I admire, "notes a goaty, rich, ripe, animal-like flavor" in a Gewürztraminer. At first, I had to think about this one. I find it hard to imagine him earnestly sniffing a goat preparatory to making his observation. Or maybe he lived on a farm or visited one and sense memory brought back the animal essence.

If Michael Broadbent takes a whiff of a ripe, fat, Rhinefelt Gewürztraminer and says, "Ah, goaty" to himself, *"Great,"* I say. It creates an instant identification of a wine using a trigger word.

Evolve your own wine-tasting vocabulary and use it!

official word designation for its ripeness. This is a lot to put on a label.

To know about German wine, you have to know a bit about their vineyard aristocrat, the Riesling grape. As I told my friend who first balked at trying a Riesling, Germany is the one place in the world where this grape hits the high notes. It's the Maria Callas of performers on its own German soil. Riesling makes delicious wines that can be really dry or really sweet. The sweet ones will be more expensive and profound but the dry ones are delicious and worth pursuing.

Dry or sweet, Riesling has style and, people say, a flowery or perfumed aroma. One can note different fruit flavors in the wine, like apricots or apples. My suggestion is to just ask for a dry Riesling, unless you want a sweeter wine.

Don't let a word trip you up. If the wine tastes "sweet," you're tasting the ripened fruit, the natural sweetness of the grapes themselves. However, if it's a good sweet wine, you don't get a sugary taste in your mouth.

You won't get really good Rieslings for $8 or $9 but you could pick one up for $20, and they're fantastic with every kind of fish dish and other foods.

Great Riesling wines from Germany have always been very popular with real wine lovers. Never mind the complicated labeling. Try one and see for yourself.

AMERICA REDISCOVERS WINE

Fifty years ago, Prohibition almost decimated the California wine industry and it was almost unheard of to drink wine socially in the United States. The wine boom started in the 1980s and was coupled with the gastronomic revolution that is still sweeping the nation.

It's hard to believe, but it was only in 1982 that the Napa Valley was officially designated a viticultural area. Twenty years ago there were a handful of wines in Napa, while today there are over one hundred fifty, or about eight hundred throughout California.

Now there's worldwide respect for American wine-making achievements. Or as one California wine maker put it, comparing American to European wine making, "How can you compare 200 years to 2,000?"

Grape growers, wine makers, and cellar masters are superstars. Their occasional appearances in New York City, the wine capital, create a buzz of fervor among the trade and the media as well as in the hearts of budding wine lovers and their more in-the-know cousins. Eager aficionados are likely to snap up well-reviewed wines at the shops like so many bargains no matter what the price.

People who five years ago thought it a sophisticated and somewhat foreign gesture to order a glass of white wine are suddenly learning how to sniff, taste, and shop for wine. So many people are making pilgrimages to Napa Valley—easily more than two million tourists to wineries a year—that traffic jams are commonplace in the once sleepy farm communities.

AMERICA

Wine is produced in nearly every state, with only a handful or so of states without a single winery. California, though, is the biggest player in the wine market and probably the state that could be credited with reigniting interest in wine and wine making all over the country. The major producing areas there range from the famous triumvirate of the Napa, Sonoma, and Mendocino counties north of San Francisco south to the Monterey or Santa Barbara areas.

Like the Gold Rush, the chronicles of the wine trade are filled with convoluted events, drama, and simple hard work. Although there were native vines growing in California, they don't make the wines we know today. The wines we drink today are made from descendants of the vines brought over in the sixteenth century by the Spanish who, when they founded the missions, also planted vineyards. Other vines were brought over from Europe about one hundred years later, and this is where the story gets complicated.

The variety of wines made in California are based on, literally, thousands and thousands of different cuttings brought here from all over Europe. This great flow of Europeans bearing vines and opening wineries occurred during the nineteenth century.

Then there was a tiny louse called phylloxera which ate through and destroyed nearly all the vines. The ravages of phylloxera were followed, in 1920, by Prohibition, when nearly every winery went under. A few wineries survived, as did their vines, resistant to phylloxera *and* Prohibition—kept open because, supposedly, they were making wines for religious orders and church sacramental purposes.

The Eighteenth Amendment, which declared Prohibition,

was repealed in 1933 after the wine industry nearly ground to a complete halt. Vineyards had either been abandoned or plowed over and replanted with other crops. Americans lost their taste for wine and many turned to spirits bought from suppliers like bootleggers or bathtub gin mills.

After 1933, which is not that long ago, Americans became cocktail crazy and didn't think much about wine. The martini was the thing. Only after World War II, really in the 1950s, which is *definitely* not long ago, wine making started up again. When you count in the years lost, you see how the American wine industry is in its infancy relative to the rest of the wine-making world. Europe's wine makers have been at it for thousands of years. They've had the time to experiment with what grew best where, how best to nurture the vines, how best to make the wine, and fulfill the potential of the *terroir.*

The American wine industry slowly started to develop and really came of age in the 1960s. In 1972 Baron Philippe de Rothschild, today part owner of a wine venture in Napa, remarked, "All American wine tastes the same. They all taste like Coca-Cola." He has, most definitely since then, drunk those words.

In the 1980's, America rediscovered wine. Within the last two decades, California wine producers have started to take things as seriously as they always should have. California was once known for the ordinary jug wines they pumped out. Things have happily changed for the better. California is producing better wines.

I like to look at the philosophy behind the wines, which is, of making California wines in California. You can't take the Cabernet Sauvignon grape and make Bordeaux in California, and you're not going to make California wine in Bordeaux. Nor should you! The grapes grow differently in California, the climate is hotter there—and, yes, there are cool-climate regions where the grapes have a more Bordeaux-like exposure—but they can only make California wines with their own distinct personality.

There's a lot of interesting wine production going on. The styles of the wines keep changing and this

> ## THE ALL-AMERICAN GRAPE
>
> Zinfandel is the all-American wine that best expresses California *terroir*. Many people think of white Zinfandel as sweet or insipid, but a good white Zinfandel is rosé-like. The white is less exalted than the red Zinfandel, which not only can be good, but fantastic.

is good. Trends change all the time, too. California wineries used to label wines with the name of the grape like Chardonnay or Pinot Noir or Cabernet Sauvignon. And although this practice is still dominant, there's also a trend toward blended wines.

AUSTRALIA

Australia's been called the brave new world of wine for a good reason: Within the last twenty years, this country's wine-making image and know-how have made it a formidable competitor in the fine-wine market. Australians not only love their wine and drink a lot of it, but they also know what they're doing when it comes to making it. They not only produce enormous quantities of wine, but so are they making giant strides in quality. Their red wines in particular are world-class: Shiraz, made from the Syrah grape and which they call Shiraz down under, is pretty much an Australian best bet. (The wine is known as Syrah in, for example, America, France, and Italy.)

In this vast country, you'd find about seven hundred wineries concentrated in a number of wine-making regions primarily spread across the southeast and southwest territories. As with grape growing anywhere else in the world, the quality of the crop and the wine it makes depends on the climate, the soil, and the commitment to quality of the growers.

Australia has no native vines. They were transported there from Europe a few hundred years ago and vintners have been experimenting with types of vines and their clones ever since. Luckily, they didn't have American Prohibition to put a monkey wrench in the wine works and set them back fifty years.

One of the great wine-growing districts is in Lower Hunter Valley, a historic area north of Sydney where the weather is warm and damp. The Syrah grape does brilliantly here and Australia is deservedly lauded for these wines. Some Australian Chardonnays from this area and other Chardonnay growing areas are of equally high quality. That hot climate imparts tropical fruit flavors with a taste profile reminiscent of many California Chardonnays.

In the cooler climates of the country, too, like the Margaret River area in the southwest tip of the country, you'll find some excellent wines. This area has microclimates similar to those in Bordeaux and this area is producing really good wines from Cabernet Sauvignon and Merlot as well as blends of these two grapes.

I usually champion the small producer, but in this case, I'd trust the commercial wine brands from bigger Australian companies. They're good, reliable standards.

Red Shiraz, though, is really their thing and what you might want to try first if you haven't had an Australian wine. With hundreds and hundreds of wine makers producing very little wine that isn't good, you'll get value for your money. The problem with Australian wine is that it can be frustrating to find the higher end wines everywhere in America. The less expensive ones, however, are more widely available to you.

NEW ZEALAND

New Zealand is also coming up strong and making a name with its biggest success, Sauvignon Blanc. This is a little two-island country determined to put its own imprint on its wines.

There are a number of wineries there, some of them huge, some of them tiny—and they all seem to be making efforts to see what works best for them. New Zealand's North Island, which is warmer, is known for its Cabernet Sauvignon and a few other red wines. They're making Chardonnay on the South Island, and of their other white wines, their Sauvignon Blanc is really wonderful. This is the same grape that proliferates in France's Loire Valley, but New Zealand's Sauvignon Blanc is a totally different style. You have to taste it to see why.

Wines from New Zealand aren't expensive and are very good quality. For such a small country, they've done a huge amount in a short time.

Recommendation: There's a wine from New Zealand that I suggest you try from a property called Goldwater Estate, Dog Point Vineyard. They make a really nice Sauvignon Blanc. It's not expensive, just under $20, and really good.

SOUTH AMERICA

South America is an immense continent and you'll find wine making in nearly every one of its countries, each with unique *terroir*. Argentina and Chile share a border and a mountain range, but these two countries stand out for me because of their interesting wines. Worldwide, Argentina, especially, is way up there among the biggest wine-producing countries—and improving in quality all the time.

The vineyards in Argentina and Chile were planted with French and other European grape varieties in the 1600s. A wide range of grapes are grown here, but if you're looking for a signature Argentine wine, get one made from their principle red, a Malbec, which is a Bordeaux varietal. They're also working with other reds like Cabernet Sauvignon, Barbera, and Pinot Noir.

Chile is trying to create an international market in a climate that ranges from the high-altitude climate of the Andes Mountains to desert orchards. Like other mountain vineyard locations elsewhere in the world, it's a very photogenic landscape. The Chilean wine makers are getting help from the French, Americans, and Italians in a push to come up to modern international standards.

Chile grows Chardonnay and Cabernet Sauvignon grapes, among others. They make very good red wine and I recently tried some of their nice inexpensive white. I wouldn't have found this white quite yet, if it hadn't been for a request from a client.

George has a wonderful, primarily French and Italian cellar of great wines. One night he called and asked, "What about wine from Chile?" He'd heard about them from a friend. I had doubts, but I agreed to find a bottle of white wine for him. Thus the good Chilean Chardonnay, which was only $10.

We tried it, George liked it, and then he asked me for something "better" to add to his cellar. In checking around, I felt the Chilean whites weren't quite ready. "I guess it's not going to replace my white Burgundy, but I'll go with it for now," George told me. I was happy that he was reaching for another wine experience, able to enjoy it, and wasn't a snob about it.

Which wine to choose from, and from which country? Each wine will be unique. The essence of wine is about where the grapes are grown and who produces the wine—the *terroir* and the passion behind the production. The variety of wines to choose from is astounding, which makes your exploration of international wines an exciting one. The best jumping-off place for you is to choose a region or a country and check on what I've suggested you sample from there. You'll enjoy them!

3

WINE, HEALTH, AND
BEAUTY

—— ❖ ——

Twice a year I go to my favorite spa in the South of France
to rejuvenate. It's not the kind of spa where you're sus-
tained on a five hundred-calorie-a-day diet or put through
grueling exercise regimens. Rather, it's a retreat where you're
expected to do as little as possible, eat fantastically delicious
meals—butter and wine always served with dinner—and undergo their famous sea water and seaweed treatment, or "thallasotherapy." The experience is transforming.

This is not elitist indulgence. In fact, you'll find an enormous cross section of people at spas like these from all walks
of life. The recommendation is that you go twice a year for at
least a week each time and undergo four treatments a day.

When you check in, you have to see a doctor. Each time
I've been there, I've seen a different doctor. This last time, I
walked into a very grand and gorgeous office overlooking the
Mediterranean and wound up being tended by the cardiolo-
gist who founded a number of these thallasotherapy centers

around France. An ex-president of the Cardiology Society of France, this doctor's ideas are not those of a food faddist or a New Age healer. They are based on convictions grounded in science. The work in thallasotherapy that distinguishes this spa is considered sound, and medical insurance in France re-imburses people for their treatments.

The doctor read the form I filled out with my medical his-tory and his first question to me was, "Do you drink at least two glasses of good red wine a day?" I assured him I did. Then he asked the all-important question, "What kind of wine?" Since I was in France, I told him, "I generally drink a lot of Bordeaux." He deemed this an excellent choice and asked me what vintages I liked best. He completed my med-ical examination chatting eagerly with me about wine. It turned out we were born in the same year, to which he added, "One of the greatest years for wines, ever!"

I was there for six days and had three meals a day. I took virtually no exercise except swimming a few laps in the pool and maybe a little treadmill walking. I did a lot of relaxing and sleeping. By the end of my stay there, I'd lost almost eight pounds without trying—but simply through the food, the wine, the treatments and the ambience. I was all alone there at a beautiful place overlooking the Mediterranean, having three-course lunches or dinners over an hour and a half, sip-ping good red wine.

My stay there once again reaffirmed my deepest convic-tions:

- Good wine is good for you.

- Wine is a source of nutrients that help sustain life.

- Wine is a *living* liquid.

Although wine is food, not a medicine, like food, wine is good for your body and your soul. As research increasingly is proving, drinking wine can really make a difference in your health.

Wine's health-giving properties really became headline news over a decade ago with a study on the phenomenon called "The French Paradox." Wine finally got the attention it deserved.

THE FRENCH PARADOX

Wine, oil, and bread were the triumvirate of deified foods in Greek mythology. With their heavenly properties, it turns out that they're still worthy of worship. We know the value of olive oil and whole grains in the diet, but what a surprise it was for most Americans to learn that wine was significant, too.

The findings that made up the "French paradox" made sense not only to the French, but to anyone living in a Mediterranean culture: The French eat a lot of high-fat cheeses and foods made with butter—about 30 percent more fat than Americans consume. When the French are tested, results show low cholesterol levels. Most interesting in the equation, they have 40 percent fewer heart attacks.

About one hundred scientific studies, which began with researchers from Denmark, made the link between diet and longer life: They found compelling evidence of the connection between moderate wine consumption and a sharp increase in health benefits. The TV news magazine show, *60 Minutes,* featured the story twice.

The French paradox is both a phenomenon and the name of a book that subsequently came out based on the

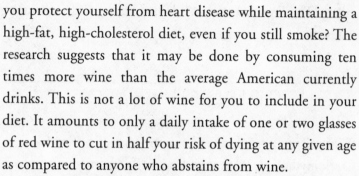

An Old Italian Proverb

One barrel of wine can work more miracles than a church full of saints.

study and promulgated the virtues of wine drinking. The gist of it is this: How do you protect yourself from heart disease while maintaining a high-fat, high-cholesterol diet, even if you still smoke? The research suggests that it may be done by consuming ten times more wine than the average American currently drinks. This is not a lot of wine for you to include in your diet. It amounts to only a daily intake of one or two glasses of red wine to cut in half your risk of dying at any given age as compared to anyone who abstains from wine.

This is amazing news: *"Ten times" the amount of wine the French drink equals one or two glasses of red wine a day for you.* Those two glasses can possibly add many years to your life. As with all alcoholic drinks, wine is meant to be drunk in moderation.

We may be discovering the healing properties of wine for the first time, but our forebears knew about them long ago.

WINE AND HEALTH THROUGH HISTORY

Hippocrates, father of modern medicine, was one of the first specialists to recognize the medicinal value of wine and prescribed it to his patients. He may not have known why exactly, but he made the crucial connection.

According to the *Encyclopedia Britannica,* many ancient

cultures learned how to convert grapes into wines, making alcohol the oldest and most widely used medicinal beverages in the history of mankind. "Alcohol" is an Arabic word, and the history of this alcoholic drink may go back to ancient Egypt from the people who also brilliantly figured out how to build pyramids and mummify kings. The Hebrew Talmud refers to wine as the foremost of all medicines, and words in the Old Testament recommend wine as both an antiseptic and a sedative. In Judeo-Christian traditions, wine became associated with holy and other important occasions and rituals. However, drinking to excess was always seen as manifestly inappropriate.

Wine was probably a result of the simplest fermentation process back then, but the effects were just as probably not so simple: Wine creates physical and psychological changes. Wine in moderation brings pleasure and too much can bring pain.

The therapeutic use of wine proliferated well into the twentieth century. Less than one hundred years ago, the *United States Pharmacopeia* National Formulary listed twelve wines it considered of medicinal quality. But with wonder drugs and new medical technologies that began developing at an astonishing pace following World War II, most of the health benefits of wine became relegated to the category of folk medicine. Wine was demoted in importance as a health tonic to the status of an alcoholic beverage made from fruit with some nutritional substance.

THE LIVING WINE

I found a quote from the *Arabian Nights* which says that wine "clarifieth the blood and cleareth the complexion and quickeneth the body and hearteneth the hen-hearted and fortifieth the sexual power in man . . ." That says it all.

The years of Prohibition in the 1920s nearly destroyed the wine industry in America, besides depriving us of our daily healthful share—from domestic or imported wines. Prohibition knocked medical interest in the therapeutic use of wine to the mat. When Prohibition was repealed in 1933, it changed the way some people thought of wine and other alcoholic drinks for the worse: They went wild and overdrank. In the 1960s, alcoholic drinks including wine were in disfavor again while recreational drugs, far more dangerous than any glass of Pinot Noir could ever be, became the norm. Then some people thought alcoholic drinks were not good for you and lobbied for warning labels on bottles of wine.

I recall a controversy in the 1970s when doctors in America worried about recommending a glass of wine to patients. Ideas about wine were different in Europe. I visited a friend who was in the hospital in England. A nurse came around at night dispensing to patients either a cup of cocoa, a glass of Guinness stout, or a glass of wine because each was considered a health boost.

We've come full circle and once again know what the ancient wine makers and their doctors accepted as true: Wine is a delicious and sensual pleasure and is also blessed with health-giving virtues.

HOW WINE DIFFERS FROM OTHER ALCOHOLIC DRINKS

People who may be a bit skeptical about wine's bounties often ask me, "Is wine better than beer or spirits, like tequila or vodka, in terms of benefits?" My answer is yes. Spirits *do not* have all the minerals, vitamins, and general immune system boosters that wine, especially red wine, has. Many of the biologically active substances other than alcohol in wine are elements like tannins, as well as powerful antioxidants like veratrole and catechin, to name only a few, that are known to reduce blood clotting and reduce risk of heart attacks.

This is important. *Moderate* amounts of red wine prevent blood platelets from clumping together and forming blood clots, whereas similar amounts of white wine or other types of alcohol do not. Epidemiological studies show that wine drinkers do better than beer and spirits drinkers in terms of surviving disease. For example, in a study of one hundred thousand adults conducted by the Kaiser Medical Center in California, one doctor found lower rates of heart disease among wine drinkers than among drinkers of other beverages.

There's a committee in Bordeaux dedicated to researching and distributing information on wine and health as part of the European Institute of Wine Health Society. One of the founding members has written a great deal on the subject. She points out that the benefits of red Bordeaux wine lies in their percentage of tannin and esocyanine, which distinguishes them from other alcoholic beverages. These components, called polyphenols, have a beneficial effect on the body's vascular system and also act as antibacterial and antiviral remedies. The American Wine Alliance for Research and Education (AWARE) also collects and promotes information on the positive affects of wine drinking.

THE NUTRITIONAL BENEFITS OF WINE

So what exactly *is* in this alcoholic drink other than those mysterious polyphenols to make it a healing drink? A glass of good-quality wine has over 500 identifiable components that combine in the body for a beneficial effect. There's a bit more value in red wine than white, but white is important too.

Red wine contains antioxidants, minerals, proteins, acids, B complex vitamins to help metabolism, and resveritrol—the substance identified in the skin of red grapes with a cholesterol-fighting factor.

A recent Harvard University study found that moderate wine drinking cuts the risk of heart attacks *for women* by 25 percent and that "most women may benefit from a single drink rather than by abstaining."

Wine is good for what ails you. It's an aid to digestion, it stimulates the appetite, and it fosters the lowering of bad cholesterol. It's been thought to help prevent or improve neurodegenerative diseases, such as Parkinson's and Alzheimer's, and help lessen the degenerative effects—and perhaps even stop—osteoporosis in women. It seems that moving into old age with a glass of wine may be advisable!

A stress reducer and relaxant, dry wine has been suggested for treating both anorexia and obesity. This apparent contradiction is explained by the fact that anxiety and emotional tension is a factor in the relationship to food, especially in the extremes of starving oneself or binging. Wine has also been used to treat the effects of food poisoning or traveler's digestive upsets. As Louis Pasteur said, and it's still true in some parts of the world, wine is cleaner than water.

As the health properties of red wine are undeniable and becoming increasingly better understood, some drug companies are trying to isolate the beneficial nutrients in wine and market them individually or as compounds.

WINE AND NUTRIENTS

For wine drinkers the key to good health may be just skin deep—grape skin, that is. What distinguishes red wine from white, among its other qualities, is that element in the grape skins, resveritrol.

Resveritrol is a key factor in wine's healing nature. Two Cornell University researchers who study fruit put the French paradox findings together with results of an obscure ten-year-old Japanese study that described the medicinal use of Japanese herbal folk remedies, including wine. These researchers made the scientific link between red wine and the reason for its cholesterol-fighting factors.

One test with red wine led to another and white wine was placed against the red wines from Bordeaux. The red wines were found to have much more resveritrol than the whites, due to the fact that red wines are fermented with their skins while white wines are fermented without them. Indeed, Bordeaux wines had the highest level of resveritrol. The level of processing also seems to have an effect on the amount.

Given the complexity of wine, with scores of aromatic compounds and numerous sugars and other scores of nutrients, there is intriguing evidence that points to the importance of a single element, potassium. Wine is very high in potassium, which has long been known to play a critical role in the electrolyte balance in the brain as well as maintaining healthy heart tissue. Not surprisingly, people with heart disease or those with severe hypertension are found to have very low levels of potassium in their systems. It is potassium that helps prevent extreme thickening of the artery walls and stabilizes blood pressure.

Wine is said to have 25 to 40 percent more potassium

than sodium, a proportion that is as high or higher than that found in many potassium-rich fresh vegetables. Regular wine drinking may be a vital source of this nutrient, especially when you realize that valuable vegetable nutrients such as potassium are lost in the cooking process.

If we're suffering from potassium deprivation, it could be because Americans have taken on a diet that's high in protein, high in sugar and carbohydrates, but low in fresh fruits and vegetables. We don't get enough potassium in our food, and red wine can help.

WINE AND STRESS REDUCTION

When I was at the thallasotherapy spa, the doctor's second question to me was, "Do you eat slowly? Americans rush through their food." I live in a big city where I see people morning, noon, or night walking down the street and eating what I know isn't a snack between appointments, but portions of entire breakfasts, lunches, and dinners. They are not having a relaxed dining experience, but are going through a speed-eating event. There may be no time during the day to slow down, but you owe it to yourself to take at least an hour, preferably two, over dinner and have a glass of wine with it. Red or white wine helps the digestion because it relaxes digestive muscles. Eating slowly ends problematic digestive complaints.

Stress reduction is vital. Wine can contribute to that.

THE MEDOC MARATHON

Let me take you back to France again. Every September you can attend the Medoc Marathon, which is run through the vineyards of Bordeaux. The marathon was the brainchild of a group of local doctors in Bordeaux who launched it about fifteen years ago, and it has remained popular ever since.

It's a hugely attended, fantastic, almost carnival-like event where people arrive from all over

> ### THE GOOD LIFE
>
> Francis Ford Coppola, the film maker, is an equally talented wine maker, bottling really good wines under his name. In an interview in the *Wine Spectator*, he says, "Fine food and wine really have almost magical properties that promote health . . . stress is the number one killer. I believe a pleasurable meal with authentic food and wine prolongs life . . . and certainly there's evidence to that effect."

the world, feeling in peak physical or psychological health. Everybody wears funny costumes and some people dress like grapes.

Instead of running through city streets, entrants jog through the vineyards of Bordeaux. Along the course there are eighteen different tasting stations of Bordeaux Grand Crus set up at each of the eighteen châteaus. People at sideline stations stand with glasses of wine to give the runners, instead of water. So you run, you stop, you have a little sip of wine, and set off again.

All in all, it's a festive event ironically flaunting excess in the hopes of confirming the idea of the beneficial role of wine when *consumed in moderation*.

This wine-drinking marathon has something in common with Americans who overexercise. Mostly, the abuse of either can be harmful to one's health. You can overdo exercise and tax the body in a mania of doing too much too often. And, as moderate exercise can increase endorphins and create a sense of calm, moderate wine drinking can lead to stress reduction.

Stress, some doctors are saying, may be the main cause of certain illnesses.

But while everyone knows exercise is beneficial to the body in dozens of ways, the stress-reducing benefits of wine are less well known. A recent study in Russia showed that stress causes the formation of biogenetic amino acids that fuel feelings of anxiety. Small amounts of wine were prescribed to people in the study, who were to drink wine with a meal during a period of ten days. The results showed an immediate effect with lowered anxiety, aggression, irritation, increase in morale and appetite, better sleep patterns, and a stabilizing of adrenalin and serotonin levels. Researchers also found that the components in wine reduced the metabolic reaction to emotional stress.

WINE AND THE COMMON COLD

Wine may not be a cure for the common cold, but it does seem to boost the immune system. This fact was an unexpected finding in a study in Britain on how stress, smoking, and other factors affect one's tendency to get colds. As a side note, they asked the test subjects about their drinking habits and if they drank wine.

The study revealed that people who drink two glasses of wine a day may still contract a cold virus. But thanks to their moderate wine-drinking habits, the cold won't be as bad or last as long as it would without wine.

Simply put, people who drink wine moderately every day may suffer from fewer colds than teetotalers.

POSSIBLE CANCER-FIGHTING PROPERTIES

Red wine also contains one of nature's most potent cancer-fighting compounds, quercetin, an element also found in garlic and onions. Studies on quercetin, including those at the University of California Berkeley and Cornell University, show that this compound has the ability to block the action of the oncogene (the cancer gene) and keep it from converting normal cells into cancerous ones. One study found that there was no increase or a slightly decreased risk of breast cancer for women who were moderate wine drinkers.

THE HEART OF THE MATTER

Wine's cardioprotective effects arise from its combination of organic compounds and trace components. Both a major Copenhagen study and a number of French studies, especially one at L'Hôpital Cardiologique near Bordeaux, substantiated that red wine lowers the level of risky low-density lipoproteins (or LDL, the "bad" cholesterol), while helping to raise the levels of high-density lipoproteins (known as HDL, or "good" cholesterol). HDL is known to lower the risk of arteriosclerosis and heart disease by cleaning the bad cholesterol from your arterial walls and helping eliminate it from the body. Essentially, red wine acts as a vascular protector and helps blood circulation through its action on LDL cholesterol (the one you don't want) thanks to its high content of what are called phenolic components (as in polyphenols, mentioned earlier).

WINE AND PEACE

"Let me confess right away, I do not drink wine for subversive purposes like improving a ratio of high density lipoproteins . . . or to just extract more nutrients. I drink wine because I like it. It makes me happy and it encourages me to like myself. Or, as someone else once said, 'No man who drank vintage port ever started a war.'"

—Hugh Johnson

The simple truth goes back again to diet: Getting consistent with red wine at meals may cut your risk of heart attack—by up to 75 percent! Switching from a high-saturated fat and starchy diet to a simple Mediterranean diet that includes red wine can also promote healthy heart function.

All the research on the benefits of wine doesn't come from international sources. "Drink red wine for your heart's content," an article in *USA Today* suggested. That red wine is better for your heart than white wine or other alcoholic beverages was stated in a report presented to the American College of Cardiology by Dr. John Solts and his colleagues in studies at University of Wisconsin. Again, they found that the natural chemicals in red wines appear to act, either on their own or in concert with alcohol, to inhibit artery-clogging by thinning the blood and preventing life-endangering clots.

This study again makes the excellent point that it is not just the alcohol in wine that affects blood tissue, but the chemistry of fermented grape juice also—and, as it would soon be discovered, the chemicals in *grape skins,* which are removed to make white wine. However, heavy drinkers and teetotalers take note.

WINE, WOMEN, AND OSTEOPOROSIS

I found an interesting study cited in an article called, "Wine May Increase Bone Mass in Elderly Women." An interesting development, this recent study on osteoporosis from EPIDOS, a medical group in France, found that drinking one to three glasses of wine per day may have a positive effect on the bone mass of elderly women, possibly reducing the risk of osteoporosis. However, consuming *more than* three glasses a day could lead to a detrimental effect on bone density.

First published in *The American Journal of Epidemiology*, this study examined the effect of alcohol by following 8,000 women aged 75 years and older; 60 percent of them did not drink alcohol at all. Among the remaining 3,000 drinkers, 1,800 were defined as light drinkers. The conclusion: Moderate alcohol use increases bone mass in the upper thighs and hipbones, showing increased mineral densities in bone tissue.

WINE AND LONGER LIFE

Since wine has such beneficial effects on the heart, on stabilizing blood pressure, possibly stopping loss of bone tissue, is replete with cancer-fighting elements, aids in digestion, and reduces stress, it is no surprise that wine is also connected to living longer.

Bordeaux wines may have been regarded as a health tonic for many centuries, and nothing proves it more than the high percentage of healthy octogenarians in the Medoc area of France—that is, Bordeaux. The number of octogenarians and even nonagenarians is much higher there than the na-

> ### GOING ORGANIC
>
> The trend in organic farming has also influenced the wine world. Some pioneering winemakers since the 1960s have gone organic, which can, for example, refer to how their grapes are grown or that their wine making process itself is chemical free.
>
> The regions of Sonoma, Mendocino, and the Santa Cruz mountain area in California are home to a number of wineries that use the word "organic" on the label. Even Fetzer Vineyards, America's sixth largest wine producer, has introduced the organic Bonterra to their huge lineup.
>
> If these wines interest you, ask at your wine shop.

tional average. It is even a local custom in Bordeaux to present a woman with a bottle of red wine before she goes into labor to help ease the birth and also bless the baby with long life.

Here is my mantra for you. Red wine . . . red wine . . . red wine. Make a daily habit of drinking red wine with dinner for the rest of your long and healthy life.

THE BENEFITS OF WHITE WINE

While most of the studies have concentrated on what red wine can do for us, researchers are beginning to pay closer attention to the virtues of white wine. And, as with red wine, there are many to make note of.

Harper's, the British wine magazine, reported on a study done by a German-Italian research team. They found that, like red wine, white wine had powerful anti-inflammatory and anticancer properties. They said that drinking white wine provided protection against cancer, osteoporosis, and arthritis. Interestingly, the researchers said it was not the *quantity* of health-giving elements in a glass of white wine that counted, but the particular type of antioxidants that were present in the polyphenols.

White wine also contains levels of elements called tyrosol and caffeic acid, both of which have significant effects on inflammatory reactions. White wine also was shown to enhance brain function by improving blood circulation and oxygen supply.

DRINKING VERSUS NOT DRINKING WINE

A glass of red wine a day keeps the doctor away. Study after study proves that a little bit of alcohol is good for you and good wine can help keep you fit. Wine is more than just a beverage containing alcohol.

Americans don't drink as much wine as their Mediterranean European cousins who have a per capita consumption of over forty liters of wine a year. Most Mediterranean cultures abide by the theory that if you drink moderately, you're likely to have a longer life.

There is moderation, and then there are the extremes:

- There's no evidence I know of that says drinking wine in moderation is harmful.

- Any drinking on an empty stomach is decidedly foolish and can be hazardous to your health. Blood alcohol levels rise half as high when wine is consumed with food. You don't want to raise your blood alcohol level but enrich your digestive, nutritional, and emotional systems with the pleasure-giving, health-giving properties that a glass of red wine will give you.

- In defining moderate consumption, I must stress that when drinking wine, never combine it with drugs—pharmaceutical, unless recommended, and never recreational.

Drinking to the point of intoxication is never correct.

Based on all the available research data, I see that *abstaining* from wine can be added to the list of health risks along with excessive drinking. It's not the amount of alcohol you drink, but the pattern of drinking that makes a difference: It takes only a very small amount of wine to help prevent heart disease, but it needs to be consumed on a regular basis. Have your glass of red wine a day—it may be more important than that apple.

Unfortunately most Americans do not have consistent and healthful alcohol consumption patterns. Many people tend to drink nothing all week and then binge drink on the weekend. In contrast, many Europeans have wine with their

---

HAPPILY, TIME CHANGES WHAT WE KNOW ABOUT WINE

The ancient Greeks believed that the only proper time to drink wine or become intoxicated was during festivals honoring the god who bestowed wine upon humanity.

Plato defined the code of desirable and undesirable behavior with the grape. He said boys under eighteen shall not taste wine at all. Wine taken in moderation may be tasted until one is thirty years old, and men (and I will include women) should stay entirely away from excessive drinking.

---

meals every day, cutting down on arterial clogging problems.

It's all about moderation and consistency in drinking wine, not an either/or—all or nothing.

The one time that abstaining from wine is perfectly acceptable is during breakfast. I've seen a lot of early-morning drinkers and it always surprises me. If you go to small towns in France, you may see farm workers on the side of the road having a glass of wine with coffee, a big croissant or a baguette, and a cigarette. If you relax and enjoy life, that's already healthy. In France they put a little wine in the water for their children, to flavor the water and to get them used to the fact that it's something that's natural to have with your meal.

THINKING OF WINE THERAPEUTICALLY

I bought one of my favorite books in France, written in French, on the therapeutic virtues of Bordeaux wines, written by three doctors who share a conviction in wine's healing powers. They've even followed up with a companion book on the therapeutic virtues of Champagne.

Just to give you an idea of its exhaustiveness, the book includes the justification, the studies, the charts, indications, and contraindications of wine. There are chapters on treating a range of disorders and diseases with wine, with suggestions on how much and how often to imbibe. Other than the subjects I touched on in this chapter (heart disease and high cholesterol, for example), there are chapters on hemorrhoids, gout, rheumatism, arthritis, and fatigue.

There are chapters on the circulatory system and health

issues related to it: anemia, heart disease, atherosclerosis, arteriosclerosis, hemorrhaging, and more. Then, under the digestive system, there are treatments for constipation, diarrhea, mucus membrane inflammation, dyspepsia, vomiting, liver diseases, low blood count, as well as respiratory disorders like pneumonia, pleurisy, and tuberculosis. Then there's the urinary system and "vino-care" of all your bodily secretions.

The doctors touch on diabetes, obesity, lack of appetite, nervous system problems, skin diseases, and even communicable diseases like typhoid and cholera. The book is an astonishing tome on what *specific* red and white wines can do. For example, they recommend red wine from the Medoc and St. Emilion regions of Bordeaux to treat anemia. For the heart, they suggest basic table wine from the Graves. For arteriosclerosis and hypertension, they suggest white wine from the Entre-deux-Mers.

For constipation, they suggest that you want three glasses a day of sweet, rich, white wine, high in glycerine, such as Sauternes. For diarrhea, they recommend a young red wine, rich in tannin, for example, a St. Emilion. To stop vomiting, try to get down a sparkling white wine. If you have a liver problem, you want a wine from the Entre-deux-Mers; for pneumonia, take the same wine warmed up and with some sugar in it.

Another book, *The Therapeutic Virtues of Champagne,* by the same three doctors, takes on a range of other disorders. There's a whole chapter on ridding oneself of migraine, depressive states, and *crise de coeur*—meaning an emotional crisis—with Champagne. Other chapters touch on everything from gynecological problems to insomnia and how different kinds of Champagne with different sweetness levels from different villages in Champagne can alleviate symptoms. It's all taken very seriously, and why not? Each wine comes from slightly different earth and growing conditions imparting different natural chemical properties.

If there's magic in wine, these doctors are the masters of seeking it.

WINE AND BEAUTY

Good health bestows beauty, and as good health requires our attention and upkeep, so does the beauty part.

I opened this chapter at a spa and will close it by taking you on another brief spa adventure. This one is named Sources de Caudalie, where the focus is on a treatment definitely worth a trial and involving wine: *vinotherapy.*

The place itself is a hotel and spa located in the middle of a vineyard on the grounds of the Château Smith-Haut-Lafitte, which makes very nice wines. It's a gorgeous place with an almost Japanese sensibility to its very French style. They serve delicious food along with a fabulous wine list. It's the perfect setting to have your wine experience, inside and out.

The spa's book, called *Health Through The Grape,* explains what the treatments are good for. They say that these treatments can prevent cancer and cardiovascular afflictions and increase internal antiaging ammunition and keep weight down.

What is it? The power of grape skins and grape seed oil applied directly to the skin.

The owners have created a line of beauty products made from grape seeds, and their products are now sold all over France, called grape-seed-polyphenol skin care. They believe these grape by-products are detoxifiers, strong antioxidants that clean your system of free radicals, and are helpful in cell renewal. They also make a grape-seed oil you can cook with.

So I took "the cure" in the form of a nutritional supplement made from stabilized grape-seed polyphenols, with evening primrose oil in it. After three months, it made a difference in both my skin and how I felt.

You can take full body treatments there made from grapes—a Merlot wrap, made of grape skins plus other ingredients. You can get a honey-and-wine wrap and a red-wine bath, which is like a hydromassage with the waters that come from the fresh springs there, with extracts of red wine and essential oils in it.

This wine bath did far more for me than make me think of the episode of *I Love Lucy* in which Lucy stomps grapes in an Italian wine barrel and winds up drenched in juice. The experience left me smiling, if not laughing. When the treatment is over, you can take a wine course or get on a bike and ride around the vineyards. The spa also believes you should be drinking while you're having the vinotherapy cure, so you're given those all-important two glasses of red wine a day.

There are other products coming out on the market that are made with various grape extracts. Cosmetic companies now using ingredients from grape leaves, extract of grape seed, the skins and seeds of the grapes, include a few from France and our own Napa Valley in California.

A famous French noblewoman once said you need to have a glass of Champagne every day to look beautiful. Clearly this isn't going to be practical for a lot of us, so maybe we should lift a glass of red wine and toast your health.

In my travels, I've heard people insist that wine is nothing but the pure fermented juice of fresh grapes with simple sugar calories that make you feel good. That's like saying professional baseball is a game played by clean-cut youths who don't smoke, drink, chew tobacco, or chase women. It's possible, but not probable. There really *could* be magic to including wine in your life.

What's really important is developing a healthy attitude about wine: Drink in moderation. Enjoy and share the pleasures of wine and good food with your friends and family. Give yourself the gift of good health and work at it every day. Let wine help you do so.

4

A Walk through
a Wine Shop

❖

I have a feeling this experience has happened to you, because it has certainly happened to me: You hear about a wine that's been touted as delicious by someone whose judgment you trust or by a wine reviewer you read in the paper or see on television. The wine is a *must buy*. You take down its name and with great expectations, go off to your local wine shop. Unfortunately, the wine is not in the bins there and the owner of the shop either has never heard of it or he can't get it.

You're frustrated, and if you have the time, you call around to other wine shops or make a few trips in person. No luck.

Let's put such wine-shop dilemmas to an end.

Before I go into detail on the actual selection of wines, and how to get the right wine when you want it, let me take you through the wine shop experience a step at a time to familiarize you with how shops are generally set up and operate. These details will maximize your comfort and confidence when buying wine—and later, in discovering wines for yourself.

THINK POSITIVE BEFORE ENTERING

I had an interesting conversation with my friend Alice who just moved. She's been in her new home for three months and she's finally getting to feel comfortable there, but she's taken some old baggage with her: her fear of wine shops.

After all our years of friendship and all my advice, Alice still holds her breath before entering a wine shop and hopes for the best. She summed it up with this most recent complaint by phone, "Shopping for wine is torture. Wine shops remind me that I don't know a lot about the subject. I wind up grabbing the same Chardonnay or Chianti I always get and rush out. If I want something different, I send Stu."

Alice dreads the wine-shop experience. That she asks her husband to shop for wine is equally unnecessary, if not self-defeating. Over the years, I've heard variations of Alice's beliefs about wine shopping from literally hundreds of people. The most important beliefs to take with you when you shop for wine are these:

- Wine shopping is about fun, *not* torture.

- Wine shopping is also an adventure. Before you walk into a store, *believe* that this shopping trip will be enjoyable and that you may learn something more about wine.

The truth is, you have the advantage.

Wine shopping puts you in the position of a buyer, with

> ### TREATS IN STORE
>
> The purpose of drinking wine is not intoxication, Rumpole . . .
> The point of drinking wine is to get in touch with one of the
> major influences of western civilization, to taste sunlight trapped
> in a bottle, and to remember some stony slope in Tuscany or a
> village by the Gironde.
>
> —John Mortimer
> *Rumpole and the Blind Tasting*

money, and the choice of whether or not to patronize that
shop. The shopkeeper wants to sell you his inventory so he
can stay in business with your sale and your repeat patronage.
You should not be made to feel the shop is bestowing upon
you the privilege of having shopped there, and for *you* to
thank *them.*

If a clerk gives you attitude, don't be daunted. You're probably not bullied at a supermarket, nor do you expect or accept
such treatment. You should no more be intimidated in the
best wine shop in town than you should be at a Price
Chopper.

Let's tear down that wine-shop wall of intimidation and
enter smiling.

TYPES OF WINE SHOPS

One wintry day not long ago, I walked to Garnet, my favorite wine shop in New York, and was surprised to see a
very dapper man pouring glasses of Champagne into little
plastic cups. The tasting samples for customers were from a

bottle of Pol-Roger Champagne, which I adore. The gentleman standing there and serving the wine was Mr. Christian Pol-Roger himself, one of the most elegant and erudite vintners from one of the oldest family producers in Champagne.

He seemed perfectly comfortable pouring his delicious wine into little disposable cups at what is, basically, a super-stocked supermarket-format wine store. Garnet's customers, who would normally not have the opportunity, got to meet an actual vineyard owner, and a good one. I thought, this is great! That taste of Champagne was delicious, even if it was served in plastic and not a classic wine flute, and Mr. Pol-Roger's presence created a sense of romance in a generally un-romantic setting.

I know that a wine maker serving his own wine is not typi-cal fare for your local wine shop, or for mine, either. Such per-sonal appearances by wine legends are bonuses, and really aren't as important to you as the day-to-day service you get there. While the wine business is still considered a classic occupation of a gentleman, taking the wine business to the public is fairly down-home. At one time or another, nearly every wine pro-ducer—no matter how large or small his winery, from the West Coast of America to Piedmont in Italy—has done the shops. Vintners consider it an obligation to present themselves and their wares (at least once) to restaurateurs and shop owners and to shake hands with the consumer in the tradition of a good politician on the stump. This was certainly true for Mr. Pol-Roger pouring his Champagne that day.

My first job in the wine business was at Sherry-Lehmann Wine and Spirits on Madison Avenue and Sixty-first Street. For a feeling of a great old wine shop, nothing compares to this place. It's got a carriage-trade Dickensian aura that brings you back to old New York. There's something about the place that makes you think of gaslights, pocket watches, and clinking crystal glasses. Owner Michael Aaron employs a small army of sales people. If you're in New York City around Christmastime, you may have to take a number at the door while you watch wine-buying fervor at fever pitch.

It was an early November morning when I first walked into Sherry-Lehmann about twenty years ago to ask for a job. I had already been to many of the less legendary wine shops around the city. The comparison between the other stores and Sherry-Lehman was instantly apparent. I always felt really comfortable in these other shops, but this particular temple of wine intimidated me. I almost couldn't get through the front door. There was a lineup of serious-looking men in coats and ties behind the counter and I was convinced they were all wine experts.

I spoke to Mr. Aaron, who told me he'd already finished hiring. I begged him for a job and he assured me I was too late. I begged some more. Finally he agreed to hire me along with the twenty-two others for the Christmas season. Then I worried that everyone would know so much more about wine than I did. Three days later when I was happily ensconced behind the counter, I realized I knew more than I thought.

I went on to become a manager of the shop.

HOW WINE SHOPS ARE SET UP

To me, Sherry-Lehmann, and especially Garnet Wines, are great wine-shopping experiences as well as very successful business operations. It helps that they're wine lovers and they

Establish a Relationship with Your Wine Shop

Since I've worked in retail sales at Sherry-Lehmann, I understand both sides of the counter, so to speak. I learned how to buy wine, but I learned the art of selling it, too. That wine shop job taught me how important it is to cultivate a *personal customer–wine shop relationship*. That "friendship" assures you of getting the most for your money and the best experience from the bottle of wine you buy.

This relationship is, for me, similar to the "rotten banana" theory of fruit buying from your average fruit stall in Paris where there is no self-service. In other words, the new or unknown customer gets the bruised bananas, while the "regulars," who have nurtured their relationship with the proprietor, get the best fruit.

You'll find many of the special little wines I've recommended in this book, and hundreds of others you can discover for yourself, in wine shops anywhere *if* you do the following:

1. Find the best wine shop in your neighborhood or town. It may take a bit of exploring, so don't settle for any old liquor or wine package store because it's convenient to where you live. The best wine shops will care enough to stock good wines.

2. Make friends with either the owner or a sales assistant in the shop who will look after you and become your personal wine guru. This guru will always give you the "choice bananas"! She or he will also get into the habit of calling you to tell you that a special shipment of super wine is being delivered and will hold a bottle or two for you.

I always walk ten blocks from my home to my favorite wine store because the owner is truly passionate about the small wine producers whose wine he sells. I could easily walk just one block, but I know that the shopkeeper there is not a passionate purveyor. Why shop there?

build an inventory by buying from the importers and producers their customers will like.

Garnet is not as glamorous as Sherry-Lehmann. Instead, the supermarket check-out style prevails in a shop with some of the best prices in town. This is where the professionals go for bargains and unusual wine finds. I've never gone away disappointed.

There are dozens of ways to familiarize yourself with your town's wine shops and how they're set up. Each usually falls into one of three classifications of wine shops that I've seen across America.

- The wine shop that loves wines and specializes in finding and selling wines from smaller producers all around the world. They may or may not also sell liquors.

- The wine shop that likes wines, but tends to feature the mass-market wines over the smaller producers. You have to take your time and search for a great buy for a good price. They almost certainly also sell liquors.

- The large wine and liquor shop in a shopping mall or highway shopping center that tends to feature mass-market wines, often stacked in cases. They also sell liquors.

What you find in each shop will most certainly be different. Shops across the country will also vary in how they set up the selling floor. Some shops are organized by

- Country. You would, for example, look in the section on France for wines of many varieties from all over that country, including those from the Languedoc or red or white wines from Burgundy.

- General flavor. The shop divides the stock into ten or twelve flavor types, such as "Fruity," "Fresh," or

"Robust." You need an idea of what they mean by each flavor group and how you think the wine will go with what you'll be eating.

- Wine type. You'd look for Chianti, or Sparkling Wines or Champagnes.

- Grape type. You'd look for wines made from, for example, Pinot Noir or Nebbiolo.

The difference between shops is the difference in finding a good wine or the wine you wanted when you left to go shopping for it.

No matter what town you may live in, I suggest that you seek out a store that primarily sells wine and is *not* just a liquor store, even if you have to get in your car to find one.

However, your local "Roadside Wine and Liquor Big Store," for example, may just be an old-fashioned liquor store with a predictable wine inventory: mass-produced, nationally advertised wine. A liquor store primarily caters to customers buying scotch, vodka, and any other hard liquor, the source of their primary sales dollar. I'm sure you've been in a store like this: There's a lot of booze on floor-to-ceiling shelves, a couple of filled wine racks, and a half dozen or so cases of wine stacked up near the door.

Research your area to find a shop whose primary interest is wine or a shop where there's more of a range. You can be surprised what you find.

I went looking for a good wine shop with my friend Sarah who lives in western Connecticut. We found a big liquor store in a highway shopping center that looked possibly promising. The shop was set up like a liquor-and-wine supermarket, and we started down the aisles. We wound up buying a really nice Syrah for only $10, but it was not easy to find. I might have voiced my enthusiasm about finding the Syrah a little loudly. A moment later, I discovered we were being tracked by a woman in a tennis outfit who had been listening in on our conversation about the way the shop was set up. She finally got up her nerve to say something to me.

"I'm going to a casual dinner party at a friend's house and I don't know what to bring," she said hopefully. "I asked the salesman in the green shirt, but he wasn't very helpful. And honestly, I hope I'm not being rude, but do you have any ideas?"

She added that she didn't want to spend a fortune and the clerk had waved her over to the area with Italian white wine. So, here was a fairly intelligent woman who has just walked into a big and, she made clear, totally confusing array of wines in row after row, rack after rack, and aisle after aisle who couldn't make a choice. I asked her a few questions. I said, "Is it to accompany dinner? How much do you want to spend? Do you think your hosts prefer white over red wine? Or what were you thinking?" After some discussion, I directed her to a red wine, the Syrah I had never tasted and had also chosen for myself. I knew this wine would be really delicious and drinkable now because it was made by a producer in the south of France with a good reputation. It was inexpensive for a well-made wine.

I told the woman, "This wine will be really enjoyable, whether you or your friends know a lot about wine or nothing about wine." That's all it took for her to understand a good bottle and feel connected to the buying process in an impersonal store. I didn't have to tell her it smells like primrose or has brilliant fruit. She was thrilled and grateful, as if I had given her the greatest gift. "Too bad you don't work here all the time!" she added.

Wine shopping starts the wine-drinking experience. No matter what kind of shop you patronize, give yourself the gift of shopping where you and your tastes are respected.

NEGOTIATING THE WINE SHOP

I promised to solve your wine-buying dilemmas, and I'll start here. I have a number of criteria for getting the best from wine shops. There are a few steps that you need to take *before you shop* and a few observations you need to make *about the shop.* If you're prepared and armed with the following information, you'll do well.

THE BIG APPLE AND THE BIG GRAPE

New York City has a *lot* of wine shops. The city is also, incidentally, the fine-wine capital of America, the center of an international wine trade, and the prime market for the wines produced in almost every state of the Union.

Paradoxically, the business of selling fine wine is very much attached to a bygone era that stems from Prohibition and was linked with bootlegging. This colorful past conjures up images of dark streets, foggy waterfronts, grade-B gangster movies, and "cement shoes." Now, in fact, it is the Federal Bureau of Alcohol, Tobacco and Firearms and the State Liquor Authority that regulate the sale of wine.

Incidentally, the cover of this book was photographed in the wine cellar of New York City's wonderful and venerable 21 Club which was, in fact, a speakeasy in the 1920s.

Finding a Recommended Wine

You may read about a wine, or have one recommended to you, but it may not be available to you in your area, or the wine shop has sold out every bottle of it. Do the next best thing which may well turn out to be the very best thing: *Look for a wine, not by its name, but by the* region *in which it was made.* This is one of the smartest ways to use your wine shop to help you find the right wine.

When you look for wines from a region, for example, from Long Island in New York State or the Loire Valley in France or from Tuscany in Italy, you are pinpointing very distinctive types and tastes of wine. This assures you of getting, if not the exact wine that was recommended to you, something equally delicious.

What Kind of Wine Do You Want?

Do as you do when you're a smart shopper at the supermarket—write down what you want on a list, even if your list contains only one item. It's a lot less efficient when you wing it, wandering in and out of the aisles trying to remember if you needed paper towels and tuna fish. The same is true for wine shopping: Write down the type of wine you want, for what occasion, and if you have them, the names and vintages of your selections.

Going prepared with a list puts you in a position of power at a wine shop. When you have a list, you won't feel like you're walking in with a deer-in-the-headlights look on your face, but with some confidence. Nothing is worse than feeling as if you're at the mercy of a sales clerk.

Suppose you want a white wine for an aperitif and a red for dinner. Write both types down. Tell the clerk what will be served for dinner, if you know. Or, you could ask for a white wine that could be served before and all through dinner because, for example, your guests prefer white wine over red. Have at least some facts written down on a piece of paper, even if you look at it and it only says, "white wine/dinner."

I hope by the end of this book you'll go to a wine shop and be specific and say, "I want a Pinot Blanc from Alsace. If you don't have that, what would you suggest that would approximate it?" Right then, the clerk recognizes that you're on the ball and know what's what.

Whose Recommendations Should You Take and When?

I remember visiting a friend down south and having a wine shop experience that wound up educating me. The salesman there had just waited on a woman and sold her a bottle of Beaujolais. Then I listened as he tried selling another woman the same Beaujolais in addition to her purchase of a Spanish sherry.

I'd tasted that specific wine and heard his pitch. He told her it had a nice chocolatey aroma, making it clear that he hadn't ever tasted it! I wanted to say, "What *are* you talking about?" but I controlled the impulse.

This step may be ornery, but I cannot omit it: If you do not know what kind of wine to buy and you ask the clerk for a recommendation, *whatever his or her first suggestion, don't take it.* Do so in a very diplomatic way by saying something like, "That's really interesting, but I had *this* in mind." At this point, name a type of wine. This empowers you and tells the clerk you have some knowledge.

I don't mean to bash sales clerks, but I know what's often happening in their minds: When you work at a wine store, you are asked to meet their priority sales goals. Even though you may come across the most accommodating wine geek who loves wine, he's still got a job to hold. I know this sounds cynical but it's not. It's reality. Perhaps the shop bought five hundred cases of Muscadet from a mediocre producer because they got a deal and they're trying to sell it as *great* Muscadet.

Merchants may actually hand their clerks what's essentially a script that helps them to pitch the wines on sale that week. So to put a fine point on it, even if you do know exactly what you want, they still may try to sell you what they're pushing. You can ask for the "Château Bobo '98" and the clerk will counter with, "That's great, but have you tried *this* white wine?" That's how shops sell wines.

Also, sales people cannot taste all the wines they sell or get a free wine education at the shop. No shopkeeper is that generous. The clerk has got to learn about wines on her or his own—which is how I learned. I invested in myself. However, the finer wine stores run wine tastings, if not every day, then at least once or twice a week. The staff gets to try a few wines, but these, of course, are the ones they're promoting. Owners want clerks to say, "I tasted it and it's really good." Of course, the tasting situation being what it is, they may say they tasted a wine that never touched their lips.

This is why you need to be empowered with information. It can only help!

WHAT MAKES A GREAT WINE SHOP?

To me, the best wine shops serve you with the following:

- Salespeople who talk about wines in a way that inspires you to buy, and who leave you feeling good about your purchase
- At least one salesperson who *is* an expert and can be called on to tell you the differences between wines and recommend a bottle that will suit your needs
- A sales crew that's simpatico with your tastes and price range, and honors them
- A shop-keeping ambiance that doesn't drive you away with intimidating winespeak or make you feel like you're intruding on some elitist domain
- A shop that's determined to make your experience there so pleasant that you're eager to come back and try something different

PRICE RANGE

This is the one of the "absolutes" you probably want to stick with.

Your priority is to get the best wine value. If you go in prepared and know your budget, you're less likely to be at the mercy of a clerk. If you say vaguely, "Do you have a nice bottle of red?" you can get into trouble. For one, you might be talked into paying twice what you had in mind.

Give yourself a price range, say from $8–12 or $12–18 and up, depending on your budget, and stick to it.

People always ask me for good wines in the $10–15 range. These are my recommendations.

Judy Beardsall's Recommended Wines for $10–15

1. Edna Valley Chardonnay (California)
2. Goldwater Sauvignon Blanc, Dog Point Vineyard (New Zealand)
3. Casa Lapostelle Chardonnay (Chile)
4. Bourgogne Blanc, Girardin (France)
5. Pinot Blanc, Trimbach (Alsace)
6. Vitiano, Falesco (Italy)
7. Montefalco Rosso, Caprai (Italy)
8. Côtes-du-Rhône "Reserve," Perrin (France)
9. Borsao Rioja (Spain)
10. Mas de Gourgonnier, Les Baux (France)

And a tip: For excellent value reds, ask for something from the Languedoc in France. There are many small producers and your shop may well carry at least one of these wines. They are always available in small quantities, so it's best to ask by region, the Languedoc, for this one rather than my giving you a name you may not find.

What You Should Know about the Information on a Wine Label

The *importer's name* on a label tells me almost as much about the wine as the name of the vineyard it comes from. There is a small number of specialty importers dedicated to seeking out wines that are the most interesting and are, invariably, good value for the money. You can't be expected to know the track record of every importer, and of course, many very good wines are handled by large importers.

You can find the name of the importer either on the back or the front of the wine label. Often, when I go to a restaurant, and I'm unsure about a wine on the list, I ask to see the bottle to check who imported it. I do the same when choosing wine in a wine shop, when I may not be familiar with a specific wine. Sometimes, you won't find the word "importer" but it will say "imported by" or a "so-and-so" (naming the importer) selection.

Here are some importers to look for which always spell quality.

- Leonardo Locascio

- Kermit Lynch

- Robert Kacher

- Jorge Ordonez

- Michael Skurnik

- Louis Dressner

- Robert Chadderdon

- Peter Weygandt

- Neil Empson

Check Out Conditions in the Wine Store

This is one of my top criteria. Conditions in a wine store can make a big difference in the taste. Notice the following when you walk in:

- How is the wine displayed? Although wine is displayed in different ways in different stores, there are signals that tell you which shops are better caretakers than others. Look around. Are most of the bottles still in boxes? In some shops, wine is case-stacked in the front of the store. Usually those are the worst buys.

- How are the wines organized? Are they displayed in a way that makes it easy for you to find what you want? Check to see if the wines are gathering dust. If they are, that means they've been sitting there too long. Basically, you want to shop where there's turnover and the inventory changes. You might even ask the owner, "Do you sell a lot of this? How long has this been here? When did it come in?"

- Is the shop cool, warm, or too warm? A warm shop is a bad sign of poor caretaking. Heat is an enemy of wine.

- Is a clerk pushing a wine that's been sitting in the window? Pass on it!

- Steer clear of big nationally advertised brands—you won't get value for your money. Remember that 50 percent of the price goes into advertising. Take a chance and look for good wines from generally smaller, interesting producers rather than those big brands.

BUYING CHILLED WINES

This is an important note: People often walk into wine shops and say, *do you have a bottle of that wine, but chilled?* Please don't! It's okay to buy a chilled bottle if there's a dire emergency. Maybe you're about to propose marriage and need that ice-cold bottle of Champagne to pop the cork while you pop the question. Or you're on your way to a dinner and your host is desperate for an already chilled bottle of white wine.

Otherwise, don't expect your bottle of white wine to be chilled when you buy it. Go home and give yourself a half hour to chill it. You don't know how long it's been sitting in the shop cooler or refrigerator. Wine should *not* be stored in the refrigerator because the cork dries out.

How Much to Buy

Should you buy a case of wine? Sure, why not—assuming you have the right conditions at home to store the bottles until they will be opened (see further details on storing wine in chapter 5).

Some wine stores offer a discount by the case and others will not. It depends on your individual store.

There's one common sense rule here: If you want to buy a large quantity of wine, take a bottle home, taste it, and make your decision. Then call them to say you want a case of the wine and for them either to deliver it or hold it for pick up. Be sure not to buy in quantity until you've opened the bottle. Don't take the store's word for its being wonderful.

Trust your palate!

5

BETWEEN SHOP
AND TABLE

❖

One fine day a client called to say the 1961 La Mission Haut-Brion she'd gotten for her husband's birthday just didn't taste right. Could she send a bottle of it to my office so I could taste it? This was one of the century's greats, so of course, I was delighted to get the bottle.

The delivery took a day or so, since she'd called me from a private plane on the way to her Caribbean retreat. It turns out that drinking this great legend of a wine on a plane was not a good idea. She'd stowed the bottles in the galley, where they were jostled and shaken, then she uncorked them and poured the delicate wine straight into glasses.

Shaken is fine for a martini, not for a great '61 Bordeaux that requires decanting preparation and procedure.

I let the wine stand for a few days, then properly decanted it. The wine was fantastic! I called her to say, "I wish you'd asked me about that wine before you got on that plane!" Older delicate wines don't like bumpy rides, which stirs up the sediment. Unless they can rest and be decanted, don't open them.

You don't have to own a private plane to nearly sabotage a good wine experience. Accidents, so to speak, also happen in the home. A friend's husband bought two good bottles of California red wine and, wanting to show off the labels, stood them on the kitchen window sill. True story; dumb choice.

Sunbaked wine goes with nothing.

And so that no other wines may suffer, I've put together what you need to know about *the very easy but critical care* of your wine from the moment you leave the store with it, to the moment you serve it. These practical steps apply to both the expensive wines you may serve at a sit-down dinner or simple bottles that go with a backyard barbecue.

There's many a potential slip before and after the cork is pulled, so I want to address any possible problems you may have.

GETTING THE WINE HOME

Do *not* put your newly purchased wine in the trunk of your car, or the back of your van, especially in warm weather. Wine doesn't like the heat in there, nor does it like being agitated.

If you have a lot of errands to run, and you know you'll be driving around, try to make the wine shop your last stop. If that's not convenient, improvise some simple protective measure, such as a styrofoam cooler with a little ice or a cold pack. Use common sense. It's like packing for a picnic: You wouldn't want the mayonnaise to turn bad in the heat.

Once you get your wine home, it's best to immediately attend to its short-term care.

SHORT-TERM CARE OF YOUR WINE

You won't buy ice cream and let it melt in the trunk of your car while you drive around doing other errands. And unless you like ice cream in liquid form, you won't park it on a kitchen counter to let it sit out until after dinner. You'll put it in the freezer when you got home from the market.

To keep wines drinkable, enjoyable, and worth what you paid for them, you also need to follow a few fairly simple and straightforward steps to ensure ideal serving conditions. Here are some universal do's and don'ts based on what wine does and does not like.

Wine does not like light. You don't have to throw a blanket over your bottles of wine, but do keep them away from direct light for any prolonged period of time. Don't keep your wine where it will be directly in the line of daylight streaming in a window or near any form of light. This creates hot and dry conditions, which wine does not like.

Wine does not like heat. It wants to be kept coolish and at a constant temperature (more on this in a moment), making heat another of its enemies. Keep wine away from the hot spots in your house the way you'd protect it from the baking atmosphere in the trunk of a car. Wine (or what will *be* wine) and heat are compatible only when the grapes are still on the vine and need sun to ripen. When wine is in the bottle, it wants shade.

Do *not* keep wine in a cabinet or rack over the stove, on top of the refrigerator (heat rises), in a system that's placed against baseboard heating, or in a room with greatly fluctuating temperatures.

I've been to grand homes where a high-priced architect

came in and designed a built-in wine storage system in the hottest part of the kitchen: right next to the stove, the dishwasher, or on a wall next to the overhead hood of a big six-burner range. This is careless. They might as well have stacked the wine in the oven and turned it on to warm.

I have seen and heard of ways people want to store wine around heat that stun me. Don't do the following either: I met with a potential client who wanted to either put a big stone fireplace in the wine cellar he was thinking of building or convert his den, which already had a fireplace in it, into a wine cellar. Interestingly, this wine-wrecking concept did not originate with him, but was the suggestion of the interior designer he hired for the project.

He was going for an "old château" look for his cellar and he thought the stone fireplace would give it an authentic touch.

I told him that some ideas about wine cellars are rather foolish and this was one of them. I'm convinced his designer saw it in a Bela Lugosi movie and probably thought the burning fireplace was an evocative detail for a future wine-cellar project he would get his hands on. No château has a fireplace in the wine cellar. In fact, no wine cellar, ancient or modern, would have a working fireplace in it, if the owner really cared about his or her wines.

Wine likes a constant temperature. It does not do well if it's stored in a place where there's more than a 10-degree swing over the course of the year. If your basement, where you've put your wine cellar, gets lows of 40 degrees in the winter and 70 plus degrees in the summer, relocate your wines and install a better temperature control system. This is not the place for them. You're probably better off putting your wines in the hall closet—unless, of course, there are hot water pipes, etc., behind one of its walls.

Wine does not like a dry place—rather it likes its air humid. It is a myth that wine likes desert air. I met with a potential client who was building a super-huge house on his vast country property, which included a private nine-hole golf course. He decided he should put a wine cellar in a space he'd also allocated as a sub-basement bomb shelter. He was practicing his golf swing on his newly mown green while talking to me.

He told me what his architect and contractor had recommended in the way of design, and I agreed with most of it. When I told him what I thought needed correction, he said, "This wine cellar business is really a crock! I don't believe in any of it, but I'm putting one in because when you live out here, you're supposed to have it."

I looked at him, dressed in a shirt monogrammed with the name of his own golf course and a hat to match. I was about to speak when he concluded his rant. "So what's the big deal here? We just have to get some dehumidification equipment and that's it!"

I could have said good-bye and walked away, but I cared what happened to the treasure trove of *wine* I knew he had waiting in storage. I didn't want the $100,000 collection to perish in the wrong environment, so I said as politely as possible, "I'm going to save you from losing your collection with what I'm going to tell you now. You want to do exactly the opposite of dehumidify. If that's what your contractor thinks, get a new one. You have to put humidity *into* the room, you don't take it out."

Jack stopped putting, then he laughed and said, "I like you, Judy. You take no prisoners." He went back to his game and I left for the city. He got a nice bit of important advice for maintaining a wine cellar he didn't even want.

Wine likes a humid or damp environment, the damper the better. Wine would be happiest in a place with 100 percent humidity. Normally a wine cellar, for ideal storage, is set at 70 percent, mostly to keep the corks from drying out.

Don't store white wine in the refrigerator for weeks or months at a time. You can leave it there for a week or so, but that is about the limit. Refrigerators are coolers, but so are they desiccators. You may think that a refrigerator is cold and moist, but it is actually a dry environment, an enemy of wine storage.

Try an experiment. Put a bottle of Champagne or wine in the refrigerator and leave it there for six months and try to pull the cork out. It will have shrunk. A week or two or a month at the most will be fine, but after that, the cork will suffer. Remember that cork is a living product from a tree that expands and contracts with humidity over time. However, a cold and dry environment won't disturb the cork overnight.

Red wines and white wines can be stored at the same temperature. Ideally at 48 to 55 degrees. If you're keeping wine for a short period of time, you can keep it in a cool hall closet or other neutral kind of place, as long as it's away from any heat or light source. I'm talking about wine that's fairly young—and that you plan on drinking over the next year. Just don't keep it in a warm or hot place or near a window.

Wine does not like vibrations. Simply: Don't put wine next to any vibrating mechanical system in your apartment, room in your house, or basement. Wine needs calm and stability and doesn't like being shaken up.

Wine is not for display purposes. It may be beautiful to look at, but wine is not a decorative object to be set out as a conversation piece. This cautionary tale will emphasize why.

I recently evaluated a cellar for insurance purposes at a house in New England built by a couple who adored wine. The cellar was made of stone walls at below ground level, perfectly cooled with just the right amount of humidity, too. I thought, "What a fabulous cellar. They love wine and it shows."

I was about to tell them so when the husband said, "I've got this fantastic bottle of 1961 Petrus. Want to see it?" Because this was one of the greatest years ever for Petrus, a very expensive red wine from Bordeaux, I eagerly said yes. Then he said, "It's right here, behind me." He moved a few inches and I saw the bottle *standing up* so that when his friends came over, he could impress them. I took one look at it and barely touched the top of the cork, when it fell into the bottle. The Petrus had been standing up on that table ledge for ten years and the cork had shrunk, completely dried out.

All I could think was, "Well, so much for your Petrus." He realized at that moment that he was facing very bad news. He blanched. Recovering enough, he managed to ask me how much that bottle was worth. It was a magnum, which in top condition was valued at about $5,000. It would still be worth at least that now if he hadn't had it standing up for a decade, more concerned with impressing others with his trophy label than preserving the excellence of the wine. I didn't say that, but I was thinking it. Instead, I told him as kindly as I could, "Honestly, it's not worth anything now." That Petrus was a treasure he'd destroyed by wanting others to know he had it.

Remember, a bottle of wine is not a trophy to be left standing up or standing out.

Wine likes to lie on its side. Or as I think of it, *lounge* on its side. Remember the fate of that 1961 Petrus on display: It

---

PULLING THE CORK:
THE SIMPLE HOW-TO AND WITH WHAT

There are a few essential accessories that will maximize your wine-drinking pleasure. A good opener, that is, *a good corkscrew,* is worth the investment.

I tend not to like the charged cartridge openers or the corkscrews with little side arms that help extract and, I think, mangle the cork. You'll find more cork bits in your glass of wine with one of these pulls. I believe in the nonfancy, waiter's corkscrew or the ubiquitous Screwpull, a brand name invented by a Houston engineer in the 1980s.

A cheap corkscrew is a waste of time and money, so buy a quality one. Get one at a good local wine store or specialty shop, not one from the supermarket. If you can't find the Screwpull, choose a corkscrew that's at least six inches long and sharp enough.

A good corkscrew goes through the cork like a knife going through butter. A quality corkscrew centers itself and helps you ease the cork out without hitting the sides of the bottle or mangling the cork.

---

stood up for years, causing the cork to shrink because it wasn't in contact with liquid. Respect your wine, no matter how much it cost, and store it on its side.

WHEN SHOULD YOU OPEN THE WINE?

Among the many questions people ask me about serving wine, none occurs as frequently as, "When should I open the wine?" or "When should I open the bottle before my guests arrive so the wine *can breathe?*" They are definitely two different questions.

Since I'm an ardent wine lover, I'm partial to every sight, sound, and smell associated with the opening of a bottle *among other people.* That popping cork is the precursor of all of the pleasures that are going to come, and I like to share it. I'd say the sound of the cork coming out of a wine bottle is both beautiful and anticipatory while the deeper sigh of a Champagne cork is romantic.

Even if I'm opening a special wine that needs decanting, I'll usually wait until my first guest arrives to start proceedings. But my advice to you is: There's no official protocol about uncorking a bottle, so do it whenever you like. If your guests are due at your house at 8 o'clock, you can be ready with your corkscrew at 5 o'clock. Either leave the pulled cork out or put it back in the bottle, unless you're serving some great, old, rare, really fragile wine, which is probably not what we're talking about here. Or wait until your guests arrive to open the bottle.

It's very simple.

The Myth of Removing the Cork to Let Wine "Breathe"

So, should you "let the wine breathe?" or as I was recently asked, "How much time should I give the wine to breathe in the bottle?" These questions are founded on the myth that wine breathes in the bottle when you pull the cork out. This simply doesn't happen. As you already know by now, the only reason to pull the cork is for your own convenience—a matter of doing it now rather than later.

You can pull the cork and then pour four or five ounces of wine into a glass. Observation tells you that now the bottle has more air space in it—the space between the shoulder and the body of the bottle. The wine in the bottle will be exposed to more air and have some small measure of opening up. However, the real place the wine *breathes* is in the glass.

This is a very important piece of oenological information: Wine breathes in two ways, most efficiently and most classically *in the glass or in a decanter,* not in the bottle. This is why you should fill a wine glass to only one-third capacity. The other two-thirds of the glass provides enough air space for the wine to open up.

When we say that wine breathes, we mean that it releases all its aromas and nuances when it's exposed to air as it comes out of a tight-fitting little container—the bottle it has been residing in. You can think of the space in the bottle that results from pulling the cork as an example in a physics lesson: The surface-to-air exposure in that space in the neck of the bottle is so minuscule that it's virtually inconsequential in terms of the wine actually breathing. Air isn't rushing in since there's not enough space for any sort of rush.

Professionals in the wine business say, "Wine needs to open up," which is why you want to pour it from the bottle to a glass. When wine opens up, it is freed from the bottle, and the genie, so to speak, releases all of its beautiful qualities, flavors, and aromas. It's the wine-bottle equivalent of rubbing the lamp. The same kind of release also happens when you pour the wine into a decanter, although decanting is done for different reasons.

DECANTING WINE

Decanting is the art of taking wine from the bottle and pouring it carefully into another container, which, in this case, is normally a decanter. I have, in a pinch, used a glass water pitcher. Ideally, the decanter itself is made of clear glass with a rounded body shape—not square, which is usually made for hard liquor, like scotch or bourbon. The two main reasons to decant wine are to aerate it—let it breathe—and to let any sediment separate out from the wine.

Sediment occurs as fine wine ages. Normally, it is the older, finer red wines that "throw sediment," a natural deposit of tannins and other dark, solidified particles. Before decanting red wines that are at least eight years old or older, you need to let the bottle stand up for a day or so to let the sediment drop to the bottom. Then decant carefully so you don't pour sediment back into the wine.

This is not to say you can't decant a very young wine, which we call "tight" and refers to its flavor. Thus, when you pour tight, young wine into a decanter, you give it room to do a little bit of stretching. Decanting young wine is not unlike stretching your arms and legs and jogging in place for a few minutes after you've been sitting in the same chair for hours. The exercise oxygenates your blood and you stretch your muscles. With wine, aeration can take some of the edge off young wines.

For me, decanting provides the added advantage of letting me see a wine's color. This is the aesthetic part of wine drinking that people rarely talk about: wine for all the senses.

Wine bottles are usually green or brown, obscuring the natural color of the contents. Decanters must be *clear* glass, and always are. The clarity showcases the color of the wine. There's the practical side to clear glass, too: You need to see how you are decanting and if you've poured in any sediment.

WHAT TEMPERATURE SHOULD WINE BE WHEN SERVED?

I recently recommended a wine to my friend Vincent, who wanted a refreshing, cooling, and rewarding drink over dinner after a tough day at the office. And it was August and hot. He prefers red, even in summer, so I gave him the names of three wines to ask for at his local wine shop, any one of which would make him happy.

The shop had one of my recommendations, a Bourgueil, a red wine from the Loire Valley in France selling for $11 a bottle. Vincent called me later on to say the wine was delicious. I asked him if it cooled him off, and if not, to drop an ice cube in his glass. He was surprised. "Ice? In a glass of good red wine?" I assured him that it was perfectly okay to use ice if he dropped it in and removed it within thirty seconds or so. No longer. He should not let the ice melt.

The alternative is to put the bottle in the fridge for twenty minutes to cool it off. Loire Valley reds can be a great value, flavorful and perfect to serve in the summer.

When desperate for cooled wines, which is perfectly possible, add ice to red or white wine over a few minutes. I'm not adverse to the practice. I once met with one of the owners of one of the great Champagne houses in France, and I saw him do the same thing. I confessed to dipping ice into wine, too, and he said, "It's okay to do . . . just don't tell anybody!"

WINE GLASSES

I had dinner recently at the house of a very sophisticated woman in the real estate business who opened a great bottle of very expensive Burgundy I'd recommended to her. I can't tell you if that wine tasted good or not because she served it in *red* glasses—perfect for a Diet Coke—but not for a distinguished ten-year-old wine that I knew cost almost as much as a night at the Waldorf. The glass was so tiny, she filled it to the top think-

PRESERVING YOUR LEFTOVER WINE

This is not about long-term custody, but of taking that lovely $15 Alsace Pinot Gris, for example, and making sure that it's perfect when you take a sip a few days after you first opened the bottle.

Like the corkscrew, this is another important piece of equipment in the form of a little wine-preserving system called a Vac-u-vin, which is a brand name. A Vac-u-vin is great for keeping your partially drunk bottle of wine fresh and drinkable after it's been opened.

It works this way: A plastic pump comes with a little rubber cork that sucks the oxygen out of the bottle—oxygen being the enemy of wine. This creates a vacuum in the bottle, preserving the wine. Then you can just put the bottle in the fridge. It's a really great thing to have.

ing that solved the issue of "one serving." I had to lean into it and delicately sip the pool around the lip before it spilled.

Moments like these raise the blood pressure of wine lovers. You don't want to laugh, you want to hit the ceiling. But of course you say nothing.

So while this woman meant to get it right—she knew exactly what to do after getting the wine delivered to her and keeping it at the right temperature—she got the *serving* of it wrong. I know she wanted to impress us with her good antique glasses by serving great white wine in them, but she overreached. Colored glass may flatter iced tea, but it fights good wine (red or white) by distorting its true color!

Remember: the color of wine is your first sensory connection to it, even before aroma and taste. Colored glass masks one of the primary parts of the wine experience. I don't want to admire the color of a glass, I want to admire the wine. To give you an idea of what I mean, it's like being asked to rave about a black-and-white photograph of an Impressionist painting. You may be able to identify the artist by the work, but the full impact of a painting's light and color, and the emotional essence of the thing, is totally missing.

I'd have been overjoyed to savor that wine in a $2 *clear* wine glass from the Pottery Barn.

I see variations of this glass gaffe all the time. Without the right glass, you won't have the best wine experience. The simple rule is:

Wine should be served in basic clear glasses in standard sizes. This is all you need. The three chief obligations of a wine glass are to be clear, rounded, and to have a stem. Could anything be simpler?

There are hundreds of variations of color in wine. If you line up six glasses of white wine they'll all be different colors. It can be like looking at paint chips where yellow is not just your idea of yellow, and white is not just white. There are a million variations and hues within the color, and it's the same with wine.

Some of the fun is comparing them. Is one a very, very pale yellow, is it a straw color, or does it have a greenish hue? There are a million different colors you can admire before the wine has even touched your lips.

I don't subscribe to the use of very folksy tumblers that look like juice glasses. They may go perfectly, for example, with the restaurant feeling in a rustic trattoria in Tuscany. The glasses are inexpensive and the wine served in them usually came out of a barrel in the cellar. That's their thing. But tumblers don't do good wine justice. Tumblers don't translate to serving good wine in America—even if you're sipping from a tumbler during the year's most gorgeous sunset and you're watching it through the picture window in your penthouse.

Holding Glasses by the Stem

There are two sound design reasons for having stems on wine glasses, chief of which is that you don't wrap your hands around the bowl of the glass. Holding the stem, not the bowl, prevents you from heating the wine with your body temperature and leaving unattractive fingerprints on the glass. Wine is meant to be savored and admired, two achievements that are attained by keeping your hands off the glass. It's not very difficult to master the skill of holding a wine glass by the stem.

What should wine glasses look like?

You can get complicated, but take the simplest route: Rely on the three standard shapes and sizes, all of which are easy to find in any shop that sells wine glasses. The 12- to 16-ounce sizes are best. It doesn't matter if the glasses are inexpensive as long as they're clear.

I'm not going to say that you need a certain glass for Burgundy or a different one for a Chardonnay. I will suggest a specific glass for Champagne—as you see above, in a flute or a tulip shape. But I will advise the following:

- A wine glass should curve in a little bit at the rim, as opposed to flaring out, to keep the aromas in and allow them to waft upwards to your eager nose. You can even, in a pinch, use the same glass for red or white wine.

- A Champagne glass should keep the bubbles in, which is why you want the flute or tulip shape that curves inward at the rim. Avoid the flat, wide-mouthed *coupe* that really looks like a sorbet dish. The *coupe* dissipates the bubbles and diffuses the aromas. That's not the idea of Champagne.

• A wine glass should have at least a 12- to 14-ounce capacity. A teeny glass with a 6-ounce capacity undersells the wine. You tend to fill up these small glasses and you don't get to smell the wine. If you have the small ones, try filling them one-third full. Even if you're drinking a plain old $5 bottle of wine, try not to fill the glass up. A wine this inexpensive should still offer up some pleasant aromas that will only appear if you do *not* fill the glass all the way up. You should pay attention to the way it smells.

• To get the aroma, you have to swirl the wine, a practice many people find either scary or pretentious. *It is a myth to think that swirling is unnecessary and pretentious.* Let's break that myth right here. Swirling helps aerate the wine and the motion of the wine in a 12- to 14-ounce glass really brings up the aroma. Swirling is also fun. The first few times you might spill wine all over yourself, but so what! It's like learning to ride a bike. You're going to fall and then you're going learn to ride and enjoy it.

FINALLY, AVOID BIG "TASTING" GLASSES

Big tasting glasses with a 24-ounce capacity can hold an *entire* bottle of wine. I prefer not to use them. You can wind up drinking more than you planned, even when you're filling them one-third full. And then another one-third full. There's an interesting psychological component to using a big glass: You don't think you're drinking more than if you'd used a 12-ounce glass.

6

WINE FOR SPECIAL OCCASIONS

❖

I follow the food magazines since I like to read how gastro-nomic experts combine food and wine. I found an article in an upscale magazine that suggested a Valentine's Day din-ner of halibut with side dishes of roasted garlic coulis and a fennel and leek dish. This dinner must have been put to-gether with the idea of what to serve when breaking up a rela-tionship. Halibut? Garlic coulis? Valentine's Day?

The anti-Valentine's Day subtext was confirmed for me when I saw the selection of wines they "helpfully" recom-mended to accompany the fish. They wrote: "We chose an excellent 1992 Erbacher Marcobrunn from Langwerth von Simmern for its elegance and fragrance, although August Eser's expansive Rauenthaler Rothenberg Riesling Spatlese 1992 would be a better match gastronomically."

By the time you exhausted yourself trying to find these wines—which would probably be next to impossible—you might never want to plan a Valentine's Day dinner at home again.

I see in this example of a special occasion dinner exactly what bothers and puzzles people about matching wine to food. Both the menu and the wine are trying *way too hard* to impress. A Valentine's Day dinner can be elegant or rustic, delicious, romantic, and more universally appealing. The wines served with it can be equally as elegant or rustic, delicious, totally accessible, and inspire passion.

Fundamentally, Valentine's Day is an occasion in the way that a birthday party, a wedding, or a Christmas open house is an occasion. Occasions invite us to leave our everyday worlds to celebrate something, bang a drum, and dress up a bit. Because I believe in drinking wine every day, for me, having a meal and a glass of good wine with a friend on a Tuesday evening is just as much an official occasion.

Many people still consider drinking wine only when they're entertaining on a big scale or having guests over. However, wine is a completely relevant part of your daily life and a valid way to celebrate the occasion of having lived another day.

This heartfelt philosophy said, I agree: Milestone occasions, whether for two people or two hundred people, definitely require planning in terms of getting the right wines for your menu. The inspiration, the romance of the occasion (even a backyard barbecue can feel intimate), deliciousness, and appeal are what includes anyone or everyone in that moment called the occasion. It takes a little effort to get it right for yourself, and it can be done!

For me, far too many judgments are made about what goes with what and why.

Where did it all begin?

MATCHING WINE WITH FOOD

Over the years, wine and food pairings pivoted on what was available and evolved to what was in fashion. Availability is not an issue for us now, since the world is a much smaller place and shipping goods is easy enough. Thus, a lingering self-consciousness about getting dinner right (being in style with the wine and the food) can put a damper on enjoying ourselves. We *can* revert a little to simpler thinking.

People didn't have rules about food and wine pairings in American colonial days. They drank beer and Madeira, because those two drinks were what they could get. Colonists either brewed the beer themselves or imported it from England. The ships brought Madeira from Portugal to make it the wine of the time. It could be dry or sweet but they drank it with everything. And if you ordered wine in a tavern, it was drawn from barrels—no bottles of wine existed then.

In Edwardian times, sweet wines were served with all the meat courses—in fact, sweet wine was even served with oysters. (American tastes would reject that and say oysters go with Champagne, Chablis, or some crisp, white wine.) Later, availability and fashion in dining eventually imprinted on us our three-course habit (the appetizer, main dish, and dessert) because that is the way hoteliers who ran their dining rooms set things up at the beginning of the century.

Which wine with what food was never really a big issue. Historically, in Italy, for example, you'd eat the local foods and drink the local wines in each area of the country—still the custom now. Each region of Italy has gastronomic and viticultural differences because the climate and terrain affect and change what grows or can be farmed. So, for example, in the cool, hilly north of Italy, you'd find a Barbera wine where the cuisine features polenta and has an earthy sensibility. Truffles are found there. The wines will have a natural affinity with the pasta or the cured ham on most tables there.

In Sicily, the crossroads of the Mediterranean, the climate is warmer and the cuisine reflects the more exotic spices of Arab and Greek influences. Drinking the wines made from the Nebbiolo grape from the northwest of Italy in Piedmont with a Sicilian dish may not make a lot of sense. The flavors in the food could blur the delicacy of the wine. But drinking a brighter Sicilian wine with a northern stewed meat or poultry dish could work well.

Then again, the concept of drinking the wine whence it comes makes perfect sense. I recommend drinking local wines with local foods when I'm in wine-making country. When I go to California, I drink only California wine—the one place where I have little interest in French or any other wine from anywhere else in the world. The spirit of the land, the climate, and the wine making all capture me. I'm like the vine, I'm in that soil and for the time that I'm there, I'm connected to that earth.

WINE-PAIRING GUIDELINES: BE CREATIVE AND DARING

To be very general about working out the food and wine pairings, I'd go by two basic guidelines: *do it by contrast* or *do it by similarity.* This means your wine will correspond by color, flavor, weight, and taste. Typically, it boils down to red wine with heavier food and white wine with lighter foods. Or the old standbys of red wine with beef, lamb, and pork and white wine with fish, chicken, and veal dishes.

Or you can treat yourself with a few wine and food pairing surprises.

WHICH FOODS WORK BEST WITH WHAT WINE?

Before I talk about ordering wines for specific occasions, I have this thought. One of the most off-putting and intimidating aspects of combining wine with food is all the chat about, for example, the tannins in or acidity of a wine clashing with this or that kind of meat or fish. This isn't to say that certain wines aren't a better choice than others. For the best wine-drinking experience, adapt the traditional rules of compatibility—use common sense.

When a nicely cooked dish goes with a nicely made wine, it's a fabulous fact of life. This is a goal most hosts go for. I'm not talking about haute cuisine with an Haut-Brion. What happens in the average kitchen plows a wide path between wine and food. If some people panic about the cooking aspect of getting a dinner together, even more will panic about matching the wine with the food.

It's time to put all apprehension aside. *It is a myth that very specific wines must be drunk with specific dishes. It's a bigger myth that says red wine only with meat and white wine only with fish.* This old standby is a pretty good general concept, but don't let it rule. Again, in general, dark-colored foods go with red wines, delicate flavors with delicate wines, and spicy foods with aromatic wines. An example would be combining certain Asian cuisine with an aromatic kind of wine like an Alsace Gewürztraminer. Try it with Chinese food. Other spicy or smoked foods or barbecue call for Zinfandel. There's nothing nicer than a fantastic, rich, robust California Zinfandel—a big, red, spicy wine—paired up with southwestern cuisine or with a hamburger.

Very, very few combinations of food and wine don't work; most wine goes with most food. Although having said that, I frankly feel the ideal accompaniment for roast lamb is a Cabernet Sauvignon-based wine, a classic coupling of flavors. But that doesn't mean you must drink Bordeaux when you have lamb. The alternatives may be a Rhône or Tuscan wine or a million other choices.

You can choose rustic wines with rustic food. If you're having a big hearty stew and you're not making a refined sauce, drink a big jolly wine. If you're cooking with a very refined sauce, drink a more refined wine.

Yes, you might not want to have a glass of Chianti with raw oysters. The flavor of the Chianti can overpower the subtlety of the oysters, but this wine might work with an all-American oyster pie. So whether it's broiled with butter or sauteed in olive oil, fish is wonderful with white wine. But that's not to say that you shouldn't enjoy salmon, for example, with red wine. The rules of companionship in wines should never be so rigid to make you hesitate to experiment.

Dessert wines are the only category that doesn't have flexible standards for drinking them. Basically, very sweet desserts don't go with very dry wine. Your palate has difficulty with this combination of sweet and not as sweet, making one seem flat and the other cloying. A great sweet dessert wine, such as a Sauternes, should really star *as* the dessert, *not with* a confection. So if someone says, "I'm serving a Château d'Yquem with the chocolate cake," pass on the cake.

Breaking a Few Rules

People often ask me about those charts that delineate wines by light, medium, and full-flavored and then what works best with which dish. If you come across a chart like this and you want to use it, okay. I'm not much a believer in those charts. If I follow

> ### Toujours Champagne
>
> Champagne is not just for caviar. Champagne is the all-purpose drink. How to dress up a ham sandwich? Have a glass of bubbles with it.
>
>

them, they limit my wine-drinking pleasure.

I've had too many interesting experiences in the company of people in the wine business or great wine collectors whose choices have surprised and delighted me. At one dinner, we were served a Champagne with every course, starting with a little cheese puff, proceeding through to venison.

The Champagne changed in style, graduating from very light and ethereal (with the cheese puffs) getting heavier into the meal. The venison course was accompanied by a really gorgeous lusty, aged, Pinot Noir-based rosé Champagne. Since I know how it feels to be stupefied with delight by six different Champagnes over one dinner, I would never advise you have Champagne only before dinner.

Other nontraditional wine and food suggestions at the top of my list begin with having white wine and cheese. There is another myth that exalts red wine, especially Port, as *the* cheese wine. I first tried this combination in France when a friend offered me goat cheese and white wine at lunch. "I know you won't believe it, but this is a fantastic combination." He was right. So whether you're eating mild cheddar or a creamy Brie, put the red temporarily to the side and reach for the white wine.

Another starter idea is having a great sweet wine at the beginning of a meal with, for example, foie gras.

Furthermore, if you believe that opposites attract, you'll understand why these combinations are great, too. As salty pretzels and ice cream or pepper in cookie dough can be a delicious, totally compatible combination, so can you play with the law of opposites with wine. One of the greatest treats is a salty blue cheese, like Roquefort, eaten with a *sweet* white wine. It can be a moderately priced sweet wine from anywhere in the world.

Dessert Wine with Great Charm

When I visit my English friends at their homes for dinner, it invariably ends with the question, "Shall we have the pudding wine?" This is a little sweet wine they serve at the end of the meal.

My hosts tend to understate what they're serving, so the pudding wine could be a $400 bottle of Sauternes or a $12 bottle of a delightful wine from Provence, such as a Muscat-de-Baumes-de-Venise.

THE SIX STEPS IN PREPARING FOR AN OCCASION

Recently, I planned a client's annual Christmas party for 190 people, the sixth time I've worked with them for this gala event. It's at their house, really on their sprawling lawn, under heated tents. The food is fantastic and elaborately prepared for this holiday sit-down dinner.

Of course, they have a great wine collection.

Over the years, I've met many of their holiday party guests. In fact, they seek me out to talk about the wine. Of them, a few really appreciate the wines served. They'll actually read the menu card that has the names of the wines on it, and it will mean something to them.

So, all in all, about 10 out of 190 guests really understand the wine or the wine and food pairings.

I've consulted with people who have vast wine cellars, tons of money, or a big budget to cover a big party. Others I worked with have a limited wine budget and say, "What's the best I can do on this amount of money?"

Money's not the only factor in buying the wine. There are six issues that you'll need to address when you plan a party:

1. The occasion itself

2. The location

3. The number of people

4. The season

5. Your budget

Once you answer these five questions for yourself, you can figure out step six:

6. How many bottles of wine should you order?

The first five points determine how you'll choose your wine. Taking them a step at a time:

1. *The occasion itself.* Why are you having the get-together?

There are traditional occasions, such as Thanksgiving, Christmas, or Easter Sunday dinner. There are parties for graduation (any level), christenings, confirmations, birthdays, and even little celebratory parties for everything from having survived surgery to promotions on the job to good-bye parties.

I know a man who celebrates the birthday of his first and favorite childhood dog, Butch, with a big bash every year. Even though Butch died forty years ago, all his subsequent dogs have also been named Butch. No matter when the later Butches were born, they get to be toasted on the first Butch's birthday and are almost equally as loved. Butch's birthday is a big family summer event involving a lot of travel for a lot of people and everyone has a great time. Hail Butch and drink Barolo, which they always serve!

If you're planning a down-home kind of party like Butch's birthday, or thinking on a grander scale, as with a wedding, you want the wine to suit the food, which suits the occasion. For a friendly family dinner in the summer, you may go with a Beaujolais. Planning wines for weddings, for example, nearly always brings up the issue of deciding between Champagne or sparkling wines. Which are the best bets? If you're on a budget, I'd suggest a great sparkling wine from the south of France or a Prosecco from Italy, most of which are superior to heavily advertised domestic brands. For the same money, or less, you can open something wonderful from the oldest sparkling-wine producer in the world whose vineyards are near the Pyrenees.

2. *The location.*   Any kind of a party requires a space. Where will you have yours?

If it's happening at your home or someone's home, then you're back to going to the wine store and buying the wine.

If your party is in a restaurant or a hall or the ballroom of a hotel, you have a number of situations to think about: Who is making the food? If it's in a restaurant, work closely with the chef to choose the wine. If the chef recommends a wine, taste it before ordering many cases of it. If the sommelier recommends a wine, do the same. You may have to buy the wine through the restaurant or make an arrangement to have your choices brought in. Don't relinquish control. Stay in charge of the food and wine choices there. It's *your* party and you're paying for it.

If the party is at a hall or hotel, who's doing the catering? Work closely with the caterer on the menu and the wines. Again, figure out the arrangements for getting the wine there.

For parties at home: Even if you have a caterer, you're in your home and you should stay in charge. *Do not leave the wine choices to a caterer or someone who is cooking for you.* You'll be the one calling the wine shop once you know your budget.

An old friend called me for advice about choosing wine for her husband's fortieth birthday party. She wanted to coordinate every course of food with wine, from hors d'oeuvres to dessert, and to get it right "this time."

For his previous birthday, Laura had relied on her caterer to choose the wine, and regretted it, bottle by bottle. It turns out that the caterer was a good cook, but she'd selected a disappointing array of name-brand wines.

This is not an uncommon occurrence. Unless they *really*

know wine, caterers should stick to cooking only and be smart enough to call in a wine expert for help.

This time, I got a copy of Laura's menu from the caterer and selected a few wonderful and lesser-known wines from Italy, which worked beautifully with each dish. I was also able to locate a great vintage wine that was made in 1961, her husband's birth year. Laura loved this idea and agreed that I should get it for her. The party was a great success.

3. *The number of people.* This is the simplest aspect of putting a party together. Who's on your guest list?

Rich or not rich, pretty much everyone across economic lines agrees that a *big* party includes twenty-five or more. When you go over twenty-five people, you're moving from a more or less intimate mix to the looser, sometimes dizzying, crowd mentality. When there are larger numbers of people, they're actively involved in chatting and gripping a glass in one hand and balancing a plate on their laps and not paying much attention to the wine.

If you're having twenty, forty, sixty, or one hundred people, you'll buy one kind of wine and go cheaper, but still good. If you're expecting twelve people for a sit-down dinner for your son's graduation, you may want to pay more for the wine. When you get to big numbers you have to think differently when you get to the wine shop.

4. *The season.* Some special-event parties require seasonally predictable weather for them to take place or they are traditionally thrown in a certain season. For example, you have an annual après-sleigh-ride dinner on New Year's Day, but this year it hasn't snowed. However, you can rename the party and carry on anyway. Or you're having a big Fourth of July family

party-reunion and it's in your backyard and/or in your air-conditioned living room.

5. *Your budget.* While most people care about what the wine will cost, paradoxically, the quality of the wine can be better than you think on a budget. Being appreciative and having a developed sense of aesthetics are not related to how much money you're willing to spend on a party. You can serve a perfect bottle of simple country wine anyone would understand and enjoy drinking. So in making your wine choice, think about buying wine that falls between the more refined tastes of a connoisseur who would understand it and the guest who sips at it randomly.

Why spend great sums of money on wine when the majority of your guests are likely *not* thinking about the wine as much as the conversation and who has or hasn't arrived? Frankly, for me, there's no short cut: Quality matters and quality will cost you either a little more or a lot more. You need to find a happy medium.

You don't want to serve low-grade jug wine you know is inferior with the first sniff. Neither do you want to break the bank on the great vintage wines, unless money is no object. And there's another issue, which goes full circle back to the type of occasion.

When I'm hired as a consultant to choose the wine for a party, I always talk about the budget in relation to the situation. You might be having a party for the PTA at your child's school. You decide on a barbecue with one or two different compatible wines. You must know your budget *on the average.* If you can spend $10 to $15 per bottle of wine, you can do really, really well.

If you want to spend $8 to $10 a bottle and you're buying

the wine yourself, you need to know how to choose it or get a recommendation from your trusted guru at the local wine shop. If you're working with a caterer, again, be sure he/she/they know about wine before you take their suggestions.

6. *How many bottles of wine should you order?* I always count on three glasses of wine per person, or a half a bottle per person. This is the Judy Beardsall General Rule of Party Wine Buying. Unless you're giving an all-night or all-weekend blockbuster party, some people will drink more than their "allotted" three glasses and others will drink less. You'll see how it averages out.

Again, if you figure a half a bottle per person, and you're having eight or ten people over, you can choose from an enormous range of terrific wines without breaking the bank. Once again, if it's a celebration, you'll probably want Champagne or sparkling wine of some kind.

This always leads to another question.

7. *The truth, Judy: How good should the wine be?* People who collect or buy great wines don't bring out cases and cases of their precious jewels when a crowd comes by. They know that serving something *pleasing* is the key. You want to serve something delicious without breaking the bank. The cost of wine can mount up, even if we're talking about a $10 bottle.

WHEN TO DRINK CHAMPAGNE

"I drink it when I am happy and when I am sad. Sometimes I drink it when I am alone. When I have company, I consider it obligatory. I trifle with it when I'm not hungry and drink it when I am. Otherwise, I never touch it unless I'm thirsty."

—Madame Lily Bollinger, when asked her opinion of Champagne

However, if the wine is pleasing, which means it's got some quality, never apologize about serving it. Don't mention or bring out the great stuff. And have a great time.

SEASONAL ENTERTAINING WITH WINE

Most of my clients love to entertain with small intimate dinners at home for four or six people, which is why having a wine cellar is so important to them. Even with a cellar full of dozens of cases, they still call me to help decide which wines to serve for an impromptu outdoor dinner on a summer night for a dozen or so friends and neighbors, or a brunch to cure the winter blahs. In this case, I may look for wine they don't have and buy it for the occasion.

One of these clients asked if I could create a handy reference for seasonal entertaining with wine and food pairings. Just as we change our wardrobe for the seasons, we can change some of our wines with the seasonal foods. Even if you don't have a wine cellar to dip into, you have a source in the form of your local wine shop. So here it is for her, and for you.

This is just a rough guide, so do not take this guide literally. It is not to say that you can only drink Tuscan wines in the autumn or that you can neither wear white nor *drink* white after Labor Day. The truth is that wines go with everything and there really are no hard-and-fast rules to worry about.

At the same time, there are certain food-wine combinations that work better than others. On a hot day/warm evening, cooled reds taste great. And perhaps on a cozy fall night with the fire going, you can enjoy a bottle of Bordeaux with your lamb chops. Just the ticket. Maybe it's true that the country veal stew at your Sunday supper party is the perfect mate for a nice Côtes-du-Rhône, but there are an infinite number of wines that would work just as well. And I guess I really would rather not like to drink a glass of vintage Port at the beach. But I would love to drink Champagne in any season.

WINTER—DECEMBER TO MARCH

For special occasion dinners and parties to celebrate Christmas, New Year's Eve, New Year's Day, or Valentine's Day:

- *Big red wines* for stews, roasts, game, and warming comfort foods, especially for those served over the Christmas holiday or on New Year's Day and even on Valentine's Day, such as French wines from the Rhône Valley like Châteauneuf-du-Pape or Hermitage or a Shiraz or Cabernet from Australia or a Zinfandel from California

- *Winter whites* such as Champagne or Sherry (dry or sweet)—in fact, Champagne with just about everything

SPRING—APRIL TO JUNE

For special dinners at home with spring lamb for Easter celebrations and lighter dishes for Memorial Day parties:

- *White wines* such as white Burgundy—St. Véran, St.-Aubin, or Bourgogne Blanc

- *Red wines* such as Bordeaux

Summer—July 4 to Labor Day

For summer picnics, barbecues and casual meals:

- *White wines* such as New Zealand Sauvignon Blanc, Pinot Blanc from Alsace, Riesling from Germany

- *Red wines* (to be served cool but not ice cold) such as Beaujolais or a Saumur Champigny from the Loire Valley and Rosé (this one should be cold) from the south of France

- *Sweet wines* for after dinner such as Muscat de Baumes-de-Venise (Rhône Valley)

Fall—Mid-September to November

Dinners at home, for Thanksgiving and heading into the colder weather:

- *Whites* such as Tokay Pinot Gris from Alsace or a Vouvray from the Loire Valley

- *Reds* such as Italian reds from Tuscany or Piedmont or California Pinot Noir

Occasions Planned Around Wine

You don't need a national holiday or family or personal event to determine the type of party. You can be inspired by a wine and construct an event based on wines. The best rule of all in wine drinking as in lovemaking is to follow your own instincts. To savor the pleasure of good wine and its natural partner, good food, think up a theme, buy your wine, and call your guests.

Historically many of the greatest wine dinners have been like this. You might choose Sherry, for example, as your party's wine focal point. Sherry is a wine of almost infinite variety—from the palest most delicate to the richest style. You can serve Sherry as an aperitif, dinner accompaniment, and as the dessert.

An American wine tailgate party is wonderful to throw in crisp autumn air or the fresh vigor of a spring day. You can serve cold salmon, a variety of patés, crunchy French bread, and smoked turkey. I've been to a Chardonnay tailgate party in a Long Island beach town and was served chicken sandwiches, various good cheeses, small cakes, and American Chardonnay. The car was packed with the food along with my friend's good (but not best) service pieces, standard $3 wine glasses that looked great, and cotton napkins. It was complete fun.

Among other wine-inspired possibilities are:

- A Napa Valley Cabernet cookout featuring Cabernet Sauvignon served with steaks.

- An Australian wine barbecue with an Australian Chardonnay and shrimp on the barbie.

- Hot summer splurge featuring rosé wine and rosé Champagne. A suggested menu might be summer clam pie, pressed grilled steak sandwich and grilled tomatoes.

You can actually start with wine then devise your party.

Every social occasion is special, and to make it even better, you should never drink an inferior bottle of wine any more than you should eat bad food. Follow your fancy and be open to new ideas for wine while keeping a level head. You can't go too far wrong with the choices you make.

Or, just drink Champagne!

7

THE RESTAURANT
EXPERIENCE

❖

A few months ago, a client called me on her cell phone from a famous New York restaurant known for its wine list. She was entertaining an out-of-town customer and, with a few minutes to spare before he showed up, she signaled the sommelier to her table. She put down the wine list and turned to him, "I'd love a fabulous red that makes an impression."

He happily obliged her, rhapsodizing about a 1989 Haut-Brion. The price? How would $1,500 be? She asked him to come back in five minutes while she thought about it, and frantically dialed my number. What did *I* think? Right then, I became the "ER wine lady" because this was definitely a wine emergency.

I told her that the restaurant was asking a four-hundred-percent markup on a wine that still needed a few more years into the twenty-first century before it would reach its full and wonderful potential. The sommelier should have known that this wine was too young to drink and that it shouldn't even have been on their list. Haut-Brion is a prestigious name and the sommelier was probably dazzled by the posh label. He was likely hoping for a big sale from my client, who seemed a little too willing to spend a lot to impress her client. Add up the cost of the bottle, tax, and a tip and we're talking nearly $2,000.

I always want my clients to have a wonderful wine experience, including in a restaurant, so I recommended the name of a splendid $50 bottle of the best French country wine I knew she and her client would enjoy with their dinner.

This true-life story brings up three key questions I tend to be asked about ordering wine when dining out:

- How do you order from a wine list?

- How much should wine cost in a restaurant and is it worth the price?

- Who is the sommelier and how do I know if I can take his or her advice?

Ardent wine lovers often choose the wine first and then ask for the menu. Wine can be the centerpiece of the meal—sometimes I'll decide what to eat based on the restaurant's wine offerings. Then again, wine is not just an accompaniment to food, it *is* food, with subtlety, body, fragrance, personality, its maker's signature qualities. And, of course, it has a natural affinity with other foods on the menu.

What makes ordering wine with dinner more complex is

this: *Most of the issues people have about wine come up in restaurants rather than at home.* I've seen masters of the universe blanch when they're handed that (sometimes) slim bound book called "the wine list"! Business virtuosos can get millions signed over to them in megadeals, but when it comes to facing a restaurant's wine choices, they're like awkward teenagers, self-conscious and afraid to say the wrong thing—that is, choose the "wrong" wine.

The dining-out-with-wine experience needn't be daunting. Let me offer you an opening note of confidence: *Take it one bottle at a time!* Some of my clients fax me a restaurant's wine list before an important dinner so I can make their selections for a special evening. Since I can't be there with you, write down some of my wine best bets to take with you when you go out. Most of all, keep your restaurant choices simple and you stand a better chance of success.

THE HEART OF THE RESTAURANT EXPERIENCE: THE WINE LIST

Your experience in a restaurant begins by defusing the fear of facing the dreaded wine list. Here's everything you need to know to take charge and make it your friend.

What follows is an adaptation from a classically assembled international wine list from a midprice New York City restaurant. In this abridged version, I've noted some points to both look for and look out for. Remember, no list is perfect. I always like to shop for the hidden bargain on a wine list.

I like the way this list is organized first by white and red wine, and under each category are the wines listed by country. Such an order has clarity and all the pertinent information well presented.

The White Wines
CHAMPAGNE AND SPARKLING WINES

Montreaux, Brut NV, Napa, CA	$ 60
Chiquet, Tradition Carte Verte, Brut NV, France	75
Perrier-Jouët, Blason de France, Brut NV, France	125
Veuve Clicquot, La Grande Dame, Brut 1993, France	165
Moët et Chandon, Epernay, NV Brut Imperial, France	60

Of all these, my choice would have to be the Moët et Chandon. It is a fair price as far as wine lists go, and it is real Champagne.

UNITED STATES

Pinot Gris, Chalk Hill, Healdsburg, CA 1998	$57
Chardonnay, "Russian River Ranch," Sonoma-Cutrer, Sonoma, CA 2000	36
Chardonnay, "Clos Electruqie Blanc," Willamette Valley, OR 1998	80
Chardonnay, "Sleepy Hollow," Talbott, Monterey, CA 1998	85

My comment on these four whites: If you have decided you want to drink American, go for the Sonoma-Cutrer at $36. It's a decent price for a reliable name brand. Once the price for a domestic white goes over $40 a bottle on a list, I move on.

FRANCE

Gewürztraminer, Domaine Armand Hurst, Grand Cru, Alsace 1998	$45
Riesling, Turckeim, Domaine Armand Hurst, Alsace 1998	21
Pinot Blanc, Barrique, Domaine Ostertag, Alsace 1999	36
Meursault, Henri Germain, Burgundy 1998	68
Vouvray Sec, "Bourillon d'Orleans," Loire 1999	30
Crôzes-Hermitage, "Les Pontais Blanc," Domaine J. Claude Fayolle, Rhône 1997	52
Pouilly-Fuissé, "Verchere," Domaine Daniel Barraud, Burgundy 1997	48
Château Graville Lacoste, Graves Blanc, Bordeaux 2000	32

There are lots of choices here. I have rarely been disappointed by an Alsace wine and here you have three. I know Ostertag is a very good producer and that the Pinot Blanc would be the most versatile foodwise. I also like Vouvray which one rarely sees on a list. One can be happy here with several good choices under $40. The white Bordeaux at $32 seems a very good option as well.

AROUND THE WORLD

Anthilia, "Donnafugata," Sicilia, Italy 1999	$24
Pinot Grigio, "Sot Lis Rivis," Ronco del Gelso, Friuli, Italy	54
Chardonnay, "Virgin," Trevor Jones, SE Australia 1999	38

The white from Sicily is one good choice here since quality in Sicily is dramatically improved and their wines are a good value. Or, for a taste of Oz, try the Chardonnay from Trevor Jones—an excellent small producer. Although this Pinot Grigio producer is a very fine one, I would resist this choice at $54. I might buy it in a shop to try it at the retail cost of probably $18–20.

The Red Wines
UNITED STATES

Merlot, Harrison, Napa, CA 1998	$72
Cabernet Sauvignon, Cafaro, Napa Valley, CA 1998	84
Zinfandel, "Lytton Springs," Ridge, CA 1998	54
Merlot, "Columbia," Castle Rock, Central Coast, CA 1998	26
(This Merlot by the glass $7.00)	

The above choices are not the greatest and surprisingly expensive. Of all these, I would head straight for Ridge Zinfandel. Ridge is one of California's classic great producers of Zinfandel. I would *be unlikely to order a $72 bottle of Merlot, especially since I don't know this producer. The $26 bottle might seem like a bargain, but there are no "bargain" Merlots in my opinion. They do offer this one by the glass, so if you're irrepressibly curious, you can try it out.*

FRANCE

Bandol, "Cuvée Longue Garde," Pradeaux, Provence 1994	$52
Crôzes-Hermitage, "Thalabert," Paul Jaboulet, Rhône 1997	47
Château Montus, Madiran, Rhône 1995	42
Chambolle Musigny, "Clos de l'Orme," Sylan Lathiard, Burgundy 1998	95

If you ever see Crôzes-Hermitage on a list, it's usually a good bet. It's a little more than I want to spend, so I might go for the Montus (it's not a Rhône, by the way, but from southwest France). But it is a very good wine for under $45, which is not bad as this list goes. The Burgundy is too expensive—you're paying for reputation of the region here.

AROUND THE WORLD

Donnafugata, "Mille e Una Notte," Sicilia, Italy 1997	$96
"Les Terasses," Alvaro Palacios, Priorato, Spain 1997	$42
Pinot Noir, "Unduruga," Maipo Valley, Chile 2000	$24
(This Pinot Noir by the glass $8.00)	

Here, the Sicilian wine is no longer a bargain and I would not be tempted at this price. I would be very tempted by the Spanish wine. Priorato is an upcoming region and Palacios is an excellent producer. The $24 wine from Chile can be sampled for fun by the glass.

WHO GETS THE WINE LIST?

I was at a tasting in Georgia and a woman said, "I don't know much about wine, but I've been reading about it—that's why I'm at your lecture. And you know what? How come they hand my husband the list in restaurants and I know more about wine than he does?"

I could only answer, "Why is the sky blue?"

That women *do not get the wine list* is a major peeve of mine. Men I go out with love telling the waiter that I will be choosing the wine." Or the waiter gives it to the man I'm with—whether it's a client, date, or friend—and he automatically passes the list to me. Then when the waiter comes back and I'm reading it and asking the questions, he does a double take.

In variations of this scenario millions of times across America, the person doing the waiting assumes that a woman cannot choose a bottle of wine off a list. It's a *myth* that women do not know how to order wine, a myth I want to debunk right here by giving women confidence and knowledge in these pages. Ideally, the list should be brought to the table and *set down,* not automatically handed to a man.

That men get the wine list ninety-nine out of one hundred times reflects thousands of years of culture, changing sociology, and male-female divisions of labor, most of which are now obsolete within our national borders.

First, the *wine business* has been a basically male preserve and an area of expertise that is considered beyond the interest of women. Women have not been given a rightful place at the table even though they've been working with wine at many levels for centuries. Women who've inherited vineyards have often improved the products made in the wineries they took over when a husband, father, or brother died. Champagne maker Veuve Clicquot—translating to "the widow Clicquot" and her eponymous bubbly—is only one example of how interested women can be in wine. And the company is still going strong.

The last twenty years have seen women wine makers come to the fore and none too soon. But it is nevertheless considered a man's domain.

Second, age-old customs often included men taking women out to dinner. She got a menu, sometimes without prices. The woman got to select her food—unless the man had something special in mind. She got to hear what he wanted to choose from and maybe, but usually not, cast a vote for or against his choice. So while dating customs predate the years of women entering the social and political playing field, it's time for a change.

Finally, many women never bothered to learn how to read a wine list, still holding to the old-time religion of letting the man be the wine expert by default. Here's hoping that this book will give women the confidence, knowledge, and wine skills they need to go to a restaurant and say, *"May I see the wine list?"* With knowledge, you're in charge. You can commandeer the situation. You'll know what questions to ask, what to think about and, ultimately, enjoy yourself.

That men know about wine and women don't is an easily

debunked myth: Since more women are in the wine business than ever before, or are making it their business to learn about wine, the wine list no longer needs to be an extension of a man's world!

Nevertheless, I have a simple nongender-related question to ask of restaurants: Why does everyone get a menu and only one person get the wine list? This is something I've never understood. I've been to restaurants that have printed their wine lists on the backs of the menus, which is a great idea. The Oyster Bar in Grand Central Station in New York City does just this, and it's fabulous, with just enough of a selection to choose from.

Somewhere during the last century, the wine list became an anxiety-provoking, agonizing challenge separated from the dining experience while one person at the table assumed the role of the connoisseur. We've all been at a restaurant when *no one* knows what to order, or on other occasions when the person in the know—male or female—isn't handed the list. My suggestion is for the waiter to say, "May I leave the wine list here for you?" and let those at the table figure it out.

HOW THE WINE LIST IS ORGANIZED

Wine listing is a minor art form that, unfortunately, can be made into a pretentious exercise in sales. The original concept of the wine list can't be faulted: A place of business serving food lets its customers know what wine they can buy by the bottle. The range of the cellar is always at the discretion of the restaurateur. Since most people eat out for the food experience, not the wine, it's really up to the restaurateur to stock his cellar with wines that complement his cuisine and his prices. It's good business, too, since as with bars or night-clubs, bigger profits are made on alcoholic drinks than on anything else.

In the old days, the wine list was handwritten on paper. Upgraded technology led to typewritten or typeset or computer-generated wine lists. I particularly dislike the wine list as presented in book form. Hardbound covers simply turn the list into something weighty. And if the wine prices are high, the book form gives the wines a certain cachet.

THE SIZE OF THE WINE LIST

No matter how vast or small their lists, many of the better restaurants have big bound books where the sheets can be pulled out and updated as their cellars change.

Whether the wine list is big or small is not the issue. A huge list is not necessarily a good list. Instead, what you want is as many details as possible about the wine. You want to see written down—for every wine listed—the producer, the vintage, and the country of origin or region and any other relevant or tantalizing details.

I find that lately, it's common for many restaurants to hand you about five to ten pages, constituting what I consider a big wine list. I don't mind the size, but I *do* mind the too few minutes I'm given to choose the wine.

Think about all the countries that are wine producers and there could easily be a page for every one of them. I find it impossible to read through such a list in a minute or two, the amount of time that lapses between their dropping off the wine list at the table and a hovering waiter with his pen poised asking for a decision. I need at least a half a minute per page for ten pages or five minutes at the least. Besides this, you're talking to the people you're with about what they are eating, which is also time consuming. *The experience with the wine list is not being sufficiently valued.*

The Categories on a Wine List

Each restaurant will organize its wine in its own way, but in general you'll find about a handful of universal variations. This way, you have the fun of figuring out the logic to their system and seeing how the wines are categorized.

Lately, there's a trend to find new and novel ways to do this, supposedly meant to be user friendly. For example, some restaurants use *categories of flavor* like "Juicy" or descriptions like "Hedonistic Fruit-Bomb" as if wine were comparable in standards to chewing gum or a lethal weapon. I know they're trying to make people more comfortable with the wine list, but it's a bit cute for me.

Some restaurants believe it's more sophisticated to organize the list *by grape varietal.* This is hopeless. Unless you are familiar with the astonishing range of flavors those grapes can taste like in an astonishing variety of wines, you're stumped. For example, how would you know what "The Nebbiolo" section means in terms of ordering, unless you're familiar with a very specific maker's wine? The Nebbiolo is a grape from the Piedmont region of Italy where wines are made from the simple to the extraordinary. So, this organization is really no help to you at all.

Some restaurants organize the list *by country.* This isn't a bad idea at all. Then you'll see under France, for example, wines from all over the country, such as a Mâcon-Villages, or Sancerre. One of the benefits of the list by country is finding the culinary match of your dinner. If you're in an Italian restaurant you might say, "Let's go with an Italian wine," rounding out a certain experience. But I bet most Italian restaurants that have cared enough to have a wine list will give you other options in French, American, Portuguese, and other wines. They know what goes with their food. There's no rule that says you have to drink Italian wine with Italian food, although sometimes it's a nice plan. You can't think about the wine list unless you think about what you're eating.

Some restaurants will organize the wine list *by regions within countries*. They'll put "France" as the overall category, then under it, list the wine-making regions like Bordeaux, Burgundy, the Loire Valley, Provence, and Champagne and tell you what they have. You won't know what grape it is unless it says so.

No matter how the list is organized, be wary of these telltale signs of an *expensive* wine list designed to separate you from your good sense:

- Wine lists that are *vague* and leave out specifics, such as the *vintage*.

- Lists that feature one producer for each region or country. You know the restaurant has made a deal with the distributor of the wines, which may not be the best wines for the price on the list. I know this from my experience of having worked in the wholesale wine business.

- Lists that promise more than they deliver. These lists feature wines that are not worth the wine-list price. I tend to find this especially true with red Burgundies, which I avoid ordering in a restaurant.

When people I have dinner with order red Burgundy, it is usually way too expensive for the experience and often doesn't taste quite right. Red Burgundies are some of the most delicate and complex wines of the world, which is also why they're some of the most fascinating and potentially thrilling wines.

If you look at a wine list and see, for example, "Gevrey-Chambertin" or "Puligny-Montrachet," they sound impressive, but the names aren't enough. When dining companions tell me, "I know that name. It's got to be good," I'm not so convinced. You can order the Puligny-Montrachet and the waiter tells you, "We don't put the vintage on the list because the vintages change."

Don't fall into this trap. Of course wine vintages change. And ordering most wines is *all about vintage,* the producer, and how it's shipped here. Half the time you're not told the vintage or what vineyard the wine is from. Vintage really matters with Burgundy because it's a difficult terrain with difficult weather for growing grapes. As a result, there aren't that many great vintages, but producers make wine every year anyway and they bottle it and sell it. If the restaurant gives the vintages within a time frame, such as '95–'96, ask which year they intend to give you. If they don't know, ask to see the bottle.

Burgundies require coddling and special handling to get your money's worth. So a red Burgundy will be no less than $50 and at only $50, not worth your dining-out dollar. If you find a generic red Burgundy, which is called Bourgogne Rouge—and it must be from the Burgundy region in France—ask the waiter to tell you who the producer is. If it's from an excellent producer and it's a good vintage, it shouldn't cost more than $30, or $10–12 in a wine shop.

My tip is: If Burgundy is *the* tough choice, there's a red

wine for which you almost always get value for money. Look under what some restaurants call the "New World" in wine, referring to Australia's and New Zealand's terrific contributions. You'll also get value for your money with wines from the south of France and southern Italy.

You have a right to get your money's worth.

Hands-on with the Wine List: First, A Few Words on Cool Waiters

I'm very old-fashioned and believe in polite waiters with good instincts. That means they're not intrusive and give you time to read the list. I don't really want to have a social interaction with the waiter, no matter how nice a person he may be. The best service in the entire world is *an invisible presence* who knows when to appear and when to disappear.

Many times a waiter brings the wine list—and stands on top of you, breathing down your neck while you make a choice. Breathe back! Waiters don't hang over you when you're picking the main dish from the menu. Don't let them rush you with the wine list. Great waiters know that the wine is as important a decision as the food course. *The wine is equal to the food, not more and not less.* It's an equal marriage. You should not have wine without food or food without wine, breakfast excepted.

Selecting from the List: Working It Out

Most people have their first encounter with good wine in a restaurant, so if it's a good experience, you'll return. Restaurants want this. The important thing is for the restaurant to create a comfort level that ends the wine-intimidation factor.

Since you'll be handed the menu and the wine list at the same time, you should be thinking simultaneously of three things that are of equal importance: what you'll eat, what others with you are eating, and what wine most likely goes with the food. If you're having fish and everyone else is going with the lamb, and you only want to order one bottle of wine, where will you make your selection from? Here's the bottom line on selection: Sometimes you look at a list and you might have wanted white wine and they have poor or uninspired choices, so you go to red. Or vice versa. Then order the food accordingly.

Usually, I recommend a white wine when there's a wide range of main courses that include fish. Meat/fowl/fish dishes are easier to find a wine accompaniment for than some foods that are more complicated a match. One of them is asparagus.

I once visited a little Italian town near the Austrian border known for its white asparagus season that goes on for a few weeks. Dinner one night at a restaurant featured an all-asparagus menu. It started out with cold asparagus, followed by an asparagus souffle and asparagus *en croute*. The main course was asparagus pasta. I can't remember the dessert but I swear I saw asparagus sorbet on the menu. It was a surprisingly inexpensive and totally delicious dinner and you would not have ordered a red wine with any course. In fact, there's a local seasonal wine called Spargelwein, meaning asparagus wine, with a picture of a bunch of asparagus stalks on the label. The wine is young and fresh, made from the Sauvignon Blanc grape and it was perfect.

Your restaurant experience should be a perfect coming together of wine and food. An aesthetic encounter. Some people (like me) may order the wine first and then say, "Let's think about the food." If I'm with a lot of people, I say, "You all chat," and turn my attention to the list; when I'm with one person, I excuse myself with, "Sorry, I have to look at the list and it will take me a few minutes."

Others do the reverse and order food first. Usually, you think about both elements, which is why they bring the menu and the wine list at the same time. Take it *all* into consideration and you'll enjoy yourself more.

Of course, you're talking to the people you're with to see what they're ordering. The first question to ask at the table is, "Is everyone drinking wine this evening?" and go from there.

Menus are in hand. Now let's find out who wants a first course. Poll the table. You know what comes next: You rarely see two people or more ever ordering the same dish. I love the idea of everyone at the table eating the same meal, from the first course on, like at home.

So, more realistically, if there are five people dining, the choices are all over the map: Two people order two different types of soup, another wants salad, the fourth, paté, the fifth, poached salmon. Is there an all-purpose wine to suit all these tastes for a first course? Absolutely!

My advice to is to go with *white* wine all around at this point—a wine that will strike a middle ground. This may sound a bit unorthodox to say that a white wine goes with all categories of food; however, I think it's just fine at this point. You can't be too obsessive about this. Just enjoy yourself.

However, salad eaters be alerted: If the salad dressing is heavy on the vinegar, it can conflict with the taste of wine.

All the following wines are good choices and have the following qualities in common: light and refreshing. They are *Pinot Blanc* or *Pinot Gris* from Alsace; a less expensive white

Burgundy such as a Bourgogne Blanc or a *Mâcon-Villages;* a *Sauvignon Blanc* from New Zealand or a *Sancerre* from the Loire Valley. (In the best of all possible situations, the restaurant has a by-the-glass offering: This is the time to take advantage of it.)

WHICH WINES WORK BEST WITH ANY MAIN COURSE?

If the main dish is meat, fish, vegetables, or pasta, there can be as many choices as people—yet it would be chummy to share one wine among the five of you. You can order any of the following *red* wines to complement all these diverse main dishes. If you're ready to change from white to red wine with this course, try these reliable well-made wines—all worth seeking out on the wine list:

- Wines of a recent vintage because of lower price and optimal condition. Look for a Beaujolais, but only a very good one, such as a Fleurie or a Morgon;

- Choose a Côtes-du-Rhône, a Rioja from Spain, or a Pinot Noir from California, all red wines.

The meal is not done yet.

DESSERT WINES

People love Champagne after a meal, but it's really better as an aperitif or served throughout dinner (or lunch). As much as we wish it were so, Champagne isn't ideal with desserts, even though the fizziness of the wine and the glamour of the bottling are so enticing. The sweetness of any dessert, particularly if it's made with chocolate, overwhelms wine. I suggest you avoid confections and do something better: Make a great glass of Port or some other dessert wine *the* dessert course.

Remember: You can ask to hold on to the wine list because you may want to order another bottle. You may be starting with a white and want to go on to a red. The point is: Feel in charge of the situation.

> ## How Many Glasses of Wine Per Bottle
>
> It's easy to figure out approximately how many bottles you need to order. You will get about six glasses of wine per bottle. Go from there. If there are two of you, it's three glasses per person, or so. If you're a table of light drinkers—considering one glass per person—one bottle will do.
>
>

Sending Back a Bottle of Wine

My rule for sending back a bottle of wine extends to spoilage, not because I just didn't like it. Few people who order wine can recognize when it's "off." In fact, few servers can tell the difference.

How do you know when a wine is not drinkable or if it's been oxidized? I'm telling you the truth on this: *Experience,* I'm sorry to say, is the only way to know for sure. Most of all, the wine doesn't taste good. With less expensive bottles, there's a greater chance that they've been lying around for a shorter time and thus less chance of spoilage. However, the flip side is that inexpensive wine is often shipped carelessly, being excessively heated in the process. I usually recommend drinking expensive wines at home where you have more control over storage conditions.

WHAT'S A HOUSE WINE?

In America, the phrase "house wine" is really obsolete. Few people even say it anymore. Instead, it has been changed to a question, as in, "What wine do you serve by the glass?" or "What's your by-the-glass pour?" However, there are occasions when the phrase is appropriate and the wine, drinkable.

The old appellation "house wine" refers to any wine ranging from delicious to dishwater. If I'm traveling in Europe and go to a little out-of-the-way restaurant, I know that most people I see will have a carafe of wine on their table—probably a house wine pulled out of a barrel in the back. I will always order that wine! It's going to be good, locally made, inexpensive, and it will complement the food. You won't sit there talking about the subtleties of the wine—it's meant to go with the menu.

Meanwhile, if you ask the waiter in a restaurant what wine they serve by the glass, you rarely get a satisfactory answer beyond, "Do you want red or white?" If they respond with, "It's a nice wine from a good vineyard we like in Oregon" or "It's a Sauvignon Blanc we like from New Zealand," then at least you know they know something about wine.

Sometimes the server goes barely beyond red or white and tells you, "We have a Merlot or Chardonnay." Now you know the server knows less than he thinks he knows about wine. Remember, Merlot and Chardonnay are types of grapes that can make really good wine or really bad wine. This is not enough information for you to order. You'll need to ask the server:

- "Where is the wine from? Is it American, Italian . . . ?"

- "Can I check the bottle out myself?" (If you think the restaurant is most likely to pour by the glass from a large jug at the bar.)

- "When was the bottle opened?" (If the waiter/sommelier tells you there is by-the-glass pour.)

Be sure they investigate and come back and give you answers. Don't be afraid to ask lots of questions about the wine you're buying by the glass. I must admit that under most circumstances, I avoid the house wine.

There are more and more restaurants that specialize in interesting wines by the glass, so of course, ask for one of these. In most places, you're better off ordering an inexpensive bottle off the list than ordering from an open jug sitting out on the bar. Who even knows when it was opened? You might luck out, but it's usually not worth drinking. You could be paying $5—or whatever they're charging you by the glass— while the whole bottle probably cost them $4. And it probably tastes like it.

ENCOUNTERS WITH THE SOMMELIER

"Sommelier" is a French word meaning wine waiter or wine steward who is supposed to be knowledgeable about wine and gifted in *leading you* to the best wine choice for your money. Wine stewards are responsible for buying the wine for the restaurant, tasting it, and being accountable to the restaurant for making money on their wine by smart pricing. Some upscale restaurants hire a sommelier who should be able enough to solve all your wine-ordering worries. Sommeliers are totally distinct from waiters.

Very few people are experts in all areas within the definition of sommelier, compared to the number of expert chefs who can cook and also run a kitchen. But a great sommelier can contribute a great wine experience to your dining out. A pompous sommelier, a little too full of himself, creates quite the opposite effect.

I want to free you from the worst effects of a sommelier. If you are faced with a difficult or pompous sommelier, just remember *they're not royalty.* If a sommelier approaches your table wearing his ceremonial hardware on a thin ribbon around his neck, it's a bad sign. This accessory, called a *tastevin,* is a prelude to intimidation. It looks like a medallion or a war medal from afar, but that object dangling on the ribbon is really a flattened silver cup which has little dimpled indentations on the bottom.

I own one. I received it when I was made a Gentle Lady of the Vine by being inducted into the Order of the Knights of the Vine.

The history of the cup refers back to the time it was invented for use in the cellars of Burgundy, preelectricity. Obviously, the cellars were very dark. When the wine makers would go from barrel to barrel to taste how the wine was coming along, they'd use the cup. The little dimples pounded in when the cup was made had a real purpose: When the candlelight hit the dimples, light was refracted off them and the vintner could see the color of the wine.

I find that when sommeliers are decked out in their cups,

it brings out bravado in attitude and is a turnoff. Really more to the point, these cups make historically interesting ashtrays. You can even buy one new at Tiffany's.

The bottom line about wine stewards is this: *What matters is what they know and how graciously they serve you.* The sommelier is there to help you and not look down on you.

You're lucky when you encounter that rare sommelier who's knowledgeable about all wines and who'll be waiting on you. Few restaurants have such a person on the staff, which is why *you* need to know more about wines going in. Of course there are great sommeliers, but first I want to help you avoid some traps.

Some sommeliers work in restaurants with snob appeal or in ones that have become tourist destinations. In both cases, I fear that the sommelier will try to sell you a bottle of over-

---

ORDERING PULIGNY OR A FEARLESS APPROACH TO MASTERING FOREIGN WORDS

I know incorrect pronunciation of, say, "Puligny" (which correctly is *Pool-een-yee),* can add to the sense of intimidation in ordering wine from a list. Not to worry! If you *can't* pronounce the names on the list, then *do not.* Simply look confidently at the server and point to your selection. He or she should say the name for you, as in, "Ah, the 1995 Lynch Bages."

Even if you're tempted to repeat after the server, do not, unless he or she speaks like a native of the country from which your wine was made. I find that 50 percent of the time the server doesn't get the pronunciation correct. You may not know that.

Incidentally, after you order your wine, your server should *not* editorialize by saying, "Good choice," or "I'd pass on that. Let me recommend a finer red from that year." This person should say, "Thank you, I'll get it." Wine servers are usually not wine experts, so don't ask for their opinions, charming as they may be.

---

priced or totally over-the-hill old wine at a ridiculous price. You have a better chance of getting a good recommendation from a simple guy in a small bistro who knows what's good and what he likes.

I was reading one of my favorite English writers on wine who has his own little rant about the worst of the sommelier experience. Hugh Johnson has a few pet peeves, such as sommeliers who bring wine in a basket or a cradle to your table, which he thinks is pretentious. (I agree.) He rails at sommeliers who arrive at your table bearing the wine "slow and stony as a butler," who "with infinite gravity" condescend to let you look at the bottle before going into his routine with the corkscrew. (Again, I agree.)

Don't worry about disagreeing with a waiter in wine steward's clothing. Some waiters have educated themselves a bit more than the others in the area of wine and are happy to demonstrate their expertise. They're *faux sommeliers* and their word should not be taken as gospel.

There's a chic and fun New York restaurant I go to frequently. They have a large wine list that's expensive and people order from it because they can afford to. However, their house wine, a Crôzes-Hermitage, is especially good and one I know I can rely on.

A waiter in this restaurant who knows I'm in the wine business always greets me effusively. He hands me the wine list and he says, "Madame! Let me suggest a really good wine," and he points to a $125 bottle. He's consistent and he has never failed to suggest a high-priced offering.

I always thank him for his advice and order the house wine. I wonder: Does he believe his suggestion is a superior wine I don't know about? I don't feel obliged to order his recommendation simply because he tells me it's "really good."

Face your waiter and decline his recommendations if you think they're too expensive or you sense that he's not the person whose suggestions you'd take. Don't worry about hurting his feelings. He's braced for this kind of rejection and it means nothing to him!

Remember, your wine experience is as important as your food experience. You have the right to ask questions of the sommelier in the same way you are entitled to tell the waiter how you want your steak prepared. You don't just say, "Bring me a steak" and leave how it's cooked up to him. So should there be a discussion about what's in the bottle of Merlot.

The word "sommelier" is about "leading you," so if you think he's leading you down a garden path, take charge. Let *him* follow *you*. He works for you—after all, you're paying him. It's his job not to be annoyed, bored, impatient, or condescending and not to suggest you're asking too many questions.

Ask those questions as you want! Have as good a wine experience as you can. Otherwise, go to a wine shop, spend less money, buy a super bottle of one of my recommendations, and stay home and have a good time with it.

Always ask to see any bottle of wine you think you'll order. If the sommelier says no, *insist*. Even if the bottle is the least expensive one on the list, it does not matter. *Your order is as important as the person who's considering spending $500.*

Don't let the wine steward make you feel wrong, ignorant, or embarrassed about what you do or do not know. Put him on the line instead—as gracefully as possible. Ask for his advice and see what happens.

Some advice is good, some is not. Until you get to know the sommelier, his tastes, and the depth of his knowledge, it's a bit of a crap shoot. I took a client to a very upscale restaurant where they have a sommelier on the staff who's

---

ORDERING WITHOUT A SOMMELIER

Do as much as you can without the help of a sommelier. Sometimes, they're pushing a certain wine the way a wine shop may be pushing one they want to unload.

They may have had a meeting that morning at the restaurant at which the manager or owner said, "We bought too much Chardonnay from the south China coast and we'd better tell everyone how great it is." I've been burned on such recommendations and they're so disappointing.

---

made something of a name for himself. That night, I decided not to choose a wine, but to ask the sommelier what he thought.

I said, "Help us choose a white. We want something different and unusual. What do you suggest?" He said, "This Viognier is really interesting. I tried it and it's really good." We ordered it. It wasn't bad, but it wasn't thrilling. I was underwhelmed with a $50 bottle of uninteresting wine. We decided to order a red since the list had a very nice selection from Italy.

I found a wine I knew would work with the food, but it was priced at $225—a bottle of Tenuta di Trinoro. My client was paying and decided to order it. The sommelier came over and I told him what I wanted. He said he hadn't tasted it and knew very little about it other than its reputation as a great wine. I knew this bottle cost $125 in a wine shop, but the markup didn't bother my client. The wine was wonderful and we both enjoyed it. I would never have ordered it had my client not encouraged it. The sommelier would never have steered me to this wine which was actually a better value in terms of markup than his selection. So much for his knowledge.

Ask the Sommelier to Tell You a Story

Sometimes the best wine steward can tell you a story about the wine or the producer. The wine steward is supposed to be leading you, and one way is by inspiration. Let me tell you what I mean.

If I were the sommelier at your table and I knew that a particular wine from Saint-Aubin in France was on the wine list, I'd tell you this story: This wine is made by a man in Burgundy who's the last vintner in his region to use a horse to plow his fields. He's the last man working there to turn over the earth between the vines not using machines. Why? It may be cheaper to use modern machinery, and it may be too expensive to keep a horse—his is named Rosalie—but this vintner follows his heart.

This Monsieur Derain has a tiny vineyard where he's fanatical about the wines he produces. He believes that the meticulous attention you pay to the growing process is crucial. Thus, Rosalie. He believes that a horse pulling a plow turns over a different amount of soil than will a machine and that the hand-drawn plow works better than machine cultivation. He can spend an entire afternoon explaining his reasoning to you.

There are no fields left in Burgundy where horses can graze because land is so valuable there, and everyone grows grapes. When Monsieur Derain's situation became a news story, all the TV crews came out to film the phenomenon of a man obsessed with handcrafted wine.

On the wine list in a restaurant, his wine goes for $25 or $30 a bottle and is going to be much more wonderful than the price tag. The village he lives in is entitled to use the name Saint-Aubin, a very underrated wine, I think. Wine from the village over the boundary lines of his property could be an ex-alted Puligny-Montrachet, which he cannot call his wine. It would be five times more expensive. But his wine can be as good as a lesser Puligny made by someone who sprays his vines with all sorts of chemicals and overproduces grape crops.

(Incidentally, that Saint-Aubin wine sells for $10–15 in a wine shop.)

When a sommelier tells you a story like this, he's brought the wine to life. It's more meaningful than saying, "It's got a buttery aroma, good acidity, or floral nuance." Instead, you connect viscerally to an image of a dedicated man with his horse and his fields.

You'll never lose if you ask the sommelier if he knows of a wine with an interesting story. The bottom line is that if they're sommeliers, they should be tapped into at least one story that can transport you. I'd rather hear about Rosalie the horse than learn that the wine smells like lavender or listen to a sommelier sound off like a wine-tasting course.

So, finally, you make a decision and order wine from the person you've not allowed to breathe down your neck or con-descend to you. You've decided what you want to eat and you're happily awaiting the service of both aspects of the table.

What to Do When They Bring the Bottle

The presentation and service is just as important as the order-ing. Let's say you asked for a bottle of Napa Valley Château Montelena and it comes to your table already opened. If they don't show you the uncorked bottle, you've got a problem. It's a matter of principle and practice. *Send the bottle back.*

Do not let the waiter or sommelier pull the cork in some distant part of the bar or kitchen and arrive at your table ready to pour. Tradition holds that they must show you the bottle so you know you're getting the wine you just ordered and not a substitute—or that it was not opened earlier in the day and refilled with something else.

Look carefully at the wine label. Take the time to check the name and the vintage. It's not uncommon for someone to make an innocent mistake, especially at dinner rush, and bring the wrong wine. When checking the label on the back of the bottle, note who the importer is (see my list of reliable importers in chapter 4 on the wine shop). If you see one of these names, you can breathe a sigh of relief because it will be good wine.

If you ordered a lesser bottle of wine and they bring you a different vintage, it probably doesn't matter. But, say you ordered a 1990 Bordeaux and they bring you a 1991. In this case, it matters a lot. Either send back the '91 and order something else or ask for a substantial price reduction. That 1990 vintage would be priced at $100 compared to the '91 at $30 a bottle.

Make sure you get what you asked for. There's no shame in asking to see the bottle, so get over your timidity about asking.

Now with the bottle in front of you:

- Check for a leaky capsule. Seepage around the neck means it may have seen poor handling or storage and it could affect the taste.

- Visually check the level of the wine in the bottle. If the level is much below the neck, it could also mean trouble.

- Feel the bottle. *This is very important,* especially in a restaurant. For red wine, the bottle should be cool, not warm to the touch. Temperature drastically affects the taste of the wine and can mean the difference between great taste and spoiled wine. The ideal room temperature for storage should be at about 50–55 degrees. White wine should feel cool, not like an ice-cold bottle of soda.

- Check the cork, which adds fun to the detective work of making sure you've got the wine you want. *Do* look at it but, of course, don't sniff it. Does the information on the cork correspond to what's on the label? Inexpensive wines may not have matching information on the cork, but there's usually a distinctive branding mark with some part of the name to prevent fraud.

Now it's time for the tasting, the most important step. The proper procedure is for the server to pour a small amount of wine into the glass of the person who ordered the wine. That person needs to do three things:

1. Look at the color. Is it clear?

2. Check the fragrance. If it doesn't smell good or clean but smells musty or moldy, send it back. There's a greater chance that less exalted, less expensive bottles of wine have been in the restaurant's cellar for a shorter time, and thus, are less likely to be spoiled. However, the flip side is that inexpensive wine is often shipped carelessly and can be excessively heated in the process.

3. Are pieces of cork floating in the wine? Don't worry about it. The server may have inserted the corkscrew incorrectly and caused a little of the cork to crumble. If you use a good corkscrew, the cork should come out in one piece. The server should know how to open a bottle of wine and use a corkscrew correctly: Put the corkscrew in at the right point in the cork where it isn't hitting the edge or in jeopardy of breaking off a piece. If there are cork fragments in the glass, fish them out. A little piece of cork never hurt any glass of wine or anyone drinking it. People get agitated when they see floating cork bits and think they should throw the glass of wine away. Only do so if the cork is totally crumbled, and covers the surface of your glass. This would mean the cork is really old and the wine may or may not be in top condition.

Finally, the magic moment arrives when the server fills your glass. This moment is my biggest concern, in capital letters: Be sure your glass isn't filled more than *one-third full.* If it's more than one-third full, you can't get the aroma and the wine can't breathe. This is not a coffee mug or a water glass for which they pace around the table and keep up the refills.

Restaurants tend to train their staff to keep on pouring. The more you drink, they conclude, the more you'll reorder. The truth is that one of the biggest, if not *the* biggest revenue producer in restaurants is wine, because of the huge markup. Therefore, while you're chatting away and having a good time, they keep filling your glass.

Instead of letting the server empty the bottle of wine you just bought in another round of refills, you may have to resort to *putting your hand over your glass.* Unless someone else at the table wants a refill, suggest the same gesture to them.

It's proper etiquette, and good restaurant service policy, to have just a couple of sips left in your glass before it is refilled. There's a reason for this. It allows you to monitor how much you're drinking. Have you ever been to a party or restaurant where you wound up drinking more than you wanted to because someone kept filling your glass before it was nearly empty?

The alternative is to stop the server and ask him, in the nicest possible way, to leave the bottle on the table and to not worry about it, even if it's white wine. Usually, they keep the bottle for you halfway across the room.

People get intimidated by the person wielding their bottle of wine. They're afraid to speak up and stop the eager refiller on his rounds. Personally, this guy can ruin my dining experience. If a hand over the glass doesn't stop him, make a direct statement, like, "Thanks, but we'll order another bottle of wine if we want one. We'll let you know." Be pleasant and firm and they'll get the picture. Most restaurants are respectful.

So that I don't have to split my concentration between my dinner companions and the happy glass refiller, I opt for letting the waiter or sommelier know how I prefer to have my wine served from the start. I make my case when I order my bottle of wine. Again, this is not unlike ordering your steak medium rare and asking for the salad dressing on the side.

Take charge and don't despair. You're there to enjoy yourself. Don't be a restaurant wine victim. Don't be bullied!

HOW RESTAURANTS PRICE WINE .

As I've noted here and there in this chapter, wine markups are big money makers for restaurants. This is good for them. To make it good for you, too, and not wind up overpaying, I have a few tips to help you:

- Beware of ordering older vintages, that is, wines that are any more than ten years old and never older than pre-1990 at the outside. Restaurants tend to mark these up the most. Since you don't know how the restaurant cellars their wines, you have no idea of the conditions they've been stored in or where they came from.

- Famous names are marked up a lot, so beware of the big guns in wine.

- In restaurants, *drink simple* to drink well. You don't need to have your finest wine experiences in a restaurant, and you cannot, in part, because of the markup situation.

Whether it's a five-star restaurant or your local bistro, all eateries have something in common when it comes to wines. The simple truth is they all play with a markup of 200–400 percent or more. The same bottle you paid $12 for in the wine shop could show up at $36 on a wine list. You could even find listed a $100 bottle of Montrachet Grand Cru priced at $500, which I did once at a place I usually like a lot.

Until restaurants change the math in this profit maker, let me pass on a few of my biggest money-saving tips on how you can beat the markup mystique and pay a reasonable price for a good bottle of wine: Eliminate wines with triple digits in the right-hand column. I don't believe in spending more than $99 on a bottle, except on the rarest occasions. The more you spend in a restaurant, the less you're actually getting for the experience. Incrementally, if you get a bottle of nice wine that costs the restaurant $8 at the wholesale level and they charge you $24, it will be a better value than a $100 wine marked up to $400.

This is the markup mystique at work. You'll actually get a better deal at the $24 level and enjoy the bang for the marked-up buck. The $100 wine just doesn't have the quality of a real $400 wine. So you actually do better ordering wines on the list for under $100.

I almost never order expensive wines in restaurants unless I know the place and I see they've got a wine I've never tasted— one I would like to try with dinner. As a rule, I'm looking for price quality and the bargain in a satisfying bottle. After all, we're out to enjoy each other's company and not to talk about the wine.

Most people will pick up the glass, toast, drink and voila! no one pays attention to the wine anymore. That's why you can spend $25 and have a good time. You'll impress people more if you can pick a great value for the money from the wine list. No, I'm not suggesting to go automatically with the cheapest.

I have a simple formula to help you connect the price with the wine:

One night I went with clients for a little bite at the bar in a three-star restaurant. I looked over the wine list and decided there wasn't a bottle that met my price/quality standards. For example, they offered a bottle of white Burgundy for $120, an off-vintage from a so-so decent producer that I know cost that restaurant $30 to buy, which is all it was worth. So even

---

THE BEARDSALL RULE-OF-THUMB RESTAURANT PRICE GUIDE

I think these are reasonable marked-up prices for good wines at any restaurant in America:

- White wines: $20 to $30
- Red wines: $20 to $40
- Champagnes: $45 plus.

There are exceptions in each of these categories depending on type of wine, producer, and vintage.

---

though my clients didn't care about the cost, I would not spend the $120. Instead, funnily enough, we had a bottle of white wine made from the Fiano di Avellino grape, from a good producer in Campania, a region near Naples. It was $40—probably marked up three times from the $15 they paid their wholesaler.

It wasn't great wine, but it was *perfect* for the occasion. It tasted delicious, it was really well made, and it was perfectly balanced. Everybody was happy and we were all getting the value out of the bottle. So seek value for money—and you'll find that you can enjoy a tastier wine for the same or less amount of money.

8

Collecting Wine, Wine Accessories, and Antiques

❖

A client called about putting together a collection of wines for her daughter to enjoy when she graduates from college. Her daughter is ten years old now, so I had to think about the wines this girl would like when she's twenty-one and thereafter!

We spent a delightful afternoon going over lists of very young wines that will have a long future development and drinking window. This woman was smartly thinking ahead and doing what many European families have done for generations—laying down wine for a child's future.

Even if you don't have a child to collect for, you can "lay down" wine for your own pleasure, interest, and wine-drinking future. Collecting wine has a few things in common with collecting, for example, vintage clothes, Chinese porcelain, or toy soldiers. As a wine collector, you need the same kind of passion for the object of your pursuit, a willingness to learn about the subject, and ardent attention in taking care of your investment—no matter how great or small the cost of each bottle you buy.

The good news is that you *don't* need the income of a movie mogul to start out. My first collection was all of *three* bottles of Rioja, a Spanish wine I loved when I started to explore wines as a way of life. I was twenty-one years old at the time, and would check around the shops to figure out what I could buy. Frankly, the French wines I wanted were too pricey for me then, but I discovered that Spanish wines were a really good value. Thus began my collecting passion.

STARTING A COLLECTION

Although it seems like it would be easy to put a collection together, it's not that simple. You need to do some homework. *It's a myth that all you have to do is walk into one fairly large wine shop and work out the details in one trip.* Rather, it will be a cumulative situation, much like putting together a wardrobe, with one or two basic pieces at a time.

Collecting wine can be great sport, but to be a winner, it also requires attention and care. How do you know if collecting wine is right for you before it becomes a

---

How Much to Buy Now

When you start a wine collection for the future, I recommend buying a bottle or two every month. If you have the space, buy a case (twelve bottles) every few months and you're on the way to building a collector's cellar.

major investment of time and money? You need to know the components of savvy wine collecting. No matter how large or small your collection, whether it's three bottles or three thousand bottles, the requirements are the same. Let me take you through the steps, one by one.

Putting Off Instant Gratification

Wine is meant to be savored and drunk and drunk at the right time. If you treat wine properly, suddenly you find that you've got this fantastic little world at your fingertips. Some wines are for now, some for a year or two from now, and some need a decade or two to mature.

If you want to open every bottle of wine as you get it, collecting is probably not for you. The phrase "instant gratification" has little to do with good vintage wines.

Why Do You Want to Start a Collection?

Before you determine to become a wine collector, answer these four key questions about your reason(s) for doing it:

- Do you love wine and want to have it for your (or a family member's or friend's) future drinking pleasure?
- Is wine collecting right for you—that is, are you a good custodian of possessions that need a little extra care?
- Do you want to collect good wines for status, or to "drink the label"?
- Do you want to collect wines as an investment and sell off your cellar when you think the time is right?

You'll find the answers to these questions as you go through this chapter.

I was once at a dinner where the hostess seated me next to an executive in the real estate business. When he learned of my profession, he lit up, reassuring me he was really interested in wine and that he always enjoys it. Then he added that his oldest friend was "a big wine man" and could always recommend the best wines to him. However, he added, he didn't understand what I did.

I started out generally telling him this:

In part, I have many private clients with whom I work on developing and maintaining a wine cellar, and/or for whom I buy wines for special occasions. This ongoingness with clients lets me share some of their history, making this connection to others a wonderful aspect of my profession. One day I can have a meeting with them about opening a dozen or so bottles for an upcoming event, for example, and we'll suddenly realize that we bought that wine eight years ago. It seems like yesterday, but now that wine is ready for drinking—and they can try a bottle tonight.

"I like my wine tonight," my dinner partner said, "especially if I bought it yesterday. I don't want it to *seem* like yesterday. What's the big deal about opening a bottle years from now?"

I wanted to be polite enough, so I tried again. I basically told him this:

Laying down wine for the future has a meaning beyond the value of the bottles themselves. This wine experience gives my clients a different perspective on the poignancy and intrinsic beauty of time passing and nature. Many wines get better over the years, and those are the wines they are tending in their cellars or closets or bins. My clients have given those wines the time they need to develop, and, at the same time, they have a new wine experience to look forward to. I've had clients who think after a year or so with a certain vintage, "It will *never* be ready to drink," but all of a sudden the bottle is ready to be opened. It can be a very emotional and even a profound experience.

"I still don't get why anyone bothers!" my now tedious dinner partner said. "We live in a society that's about instant gratification, so what's the point of having a wine cellar?"

Forced by the seating arrangement to continue to answer these preposterous statements, I persevered. It takes a vineyard years and years to produce the fruit to make a great bottle of wine. Cellaring wine is never about instant gratification, but about savoring the grapes, even about the beauty of the landscape on which they grew and the nutritional blessings that wines give us as a food. Wine reminds us about the marvelous things in life.

Paradoxically, I said, most wines are meant to be drunk not long after they're bottled. You may pick up ready-to-drink, simple country wine in a shop, but more complex wines need time in the cellar. The wines I find the most delicious need time to mature, even if it's only a couple of years, which go by in a flash. Those wines will taste as good as they were meant to taste if you give them time to grow up.

If you get the passion for it, you can quickly reach a more sophisticated level of collecting, even if you never planned it that way. That is, you find yourself buying quantities of wine that are *not* ready to drink now, but by the time they *are,* they're not available on the market. This is one very good reason to have a cellar. You want to make sure you have the wines now that you can enjoy later.

So my dinner partner may never comprehend why great wines take time, and that is truly too bad. For him there is only instant gratification. That's okay in its way, but it's not the whole story.

You, too, may have a day when you want instant gratification and not want to wait a year or more for wine from *that* bottle, whatever it is. In that case, you can always buy Champagne, my all-purpose wine.

However, there's something transforming about crossing that "need" line, having your own little stash (or your great big stash) and retrieving a bottle of red (or white) wine you bought some time in the past and is now at its peak. And you are about to enjoy it.

Ultimately there are three reasons to collect wine: pleasure, pleasure, and pleasure.

STARTING YOUR COLLECTION: A FEW GROUND RULES

In terms of collecting wines, I tend to think in terms of short-, medium-, and long-term cellars. If you put together a little collection, do it with some wines that will give you pleasure *now,* some that you can enjoy in the next year or two, and others that will hold for ten or twenty years, or more.

Start small and try it out. Buy one case (one dozen bottles) or even one bottle. Great wine becomes a part of you and changes you forever and collecting is one way to keep it around.

Give your wine the care it needs so you do not ruin what you've bought.

HOW TO CREATE A MINICELLAR

You don't need a vast amount of space, such as part or all of a room in your house or part or all of a basement, to store your collection. You can begin your own personal, basic, little minicellar anywhere you can control the amount of light, heat, and humidity. For example, you want your minicellar to be *immediately accessible* as a wine source. (Remember the health benefits in a glass of wine. You want to drink one or two glasses a day.) It's nice to open a hall closet, or go to a former guest room-den or downstairs workroom, or wherever you decide on, and pick a bottle that you bought six months or six years ago. If it's time to drink it, savor it!

A minicellar is helpful because it's a time saver—you don't have to run to the store and figure out what to buy. It's like having a larder with

---

JUDY BEARDSALL'S SAMPLE STARTER CELLAR

You can start a wine cellar with twelve good bottles of affordable wines. You don't have to be rich or have a special room or designated area of the house to store them. These interesting and lively bottles fit any bill.

5 Bottles of White Wine

- 2 bottles of Champagne: a brut non-vintage from Bollinger, Pol-Roger, or any of the top houses.
- 2 bottles of Alsace Riesling: You never know when you will need a good glass of white.
- 1 bottle of sweet wine: Sauternes means instant elegance. In France they sometimes offer a glass before dinner. I may have it instead of a dessert. It also is fabulous with a blue cheese.

7 Bottles of Red Wine

- 2 bottles of Rioja: Look for good producers like Muga or Remelluri.
- 3 bottles from various regions in Italy: such as Tuscany, Piedmont, or Sicily for interesting new wines.
- 2 bottles of Bordeaux: This is the classic section of your cellar. Seek out recent good vintages from the 1990s. I tend not to look for bargains in Bordeaux, but I try to buy from the top châteaux. Ask your wine shop for their suggestions.

all the staples in it. If you want to make a bowl of spaghetti, you've got the dried pasta, a can of tomatoes, and the good quality olive oil you need—and a nice bottle of Tuscan wine to accompany the food at your fingertips. It's a really nice feeling of satisfaction knowing you have a bottle or more ready to be opened.

Although I cellar my wines in a special storage facility that's constructed for that purpose alone, I also have a version of a minicellar in my kitchen. There's an ancient little cooling larder set in under the windowsill that extends to the outside wall, fitted much like air conditioners are built into walls now.

I have a nice little mixed collection of wines in there. It makes me very happy to know that it's at my fingertips. If I decide on an impromptu supper, I can go to my minicellar and get what's right for that night.

Once you realize what it takes to keep your wines in optimal conditions, *it's not that big a deal to keep them up.* And it's fun because you have to go shopping to replenish your on-hand collection. You just need to check that conditions are right and make whatever adjustment is needed. Because the right conditions are critical to keeping your wine drinkable and worth what you paid for them, or more, let me sum up the basic do's and don'ts of care I talked about earlier in chapter 5:

- Don't keep your wine where it will be directly in the line of daylight streaming in a window or near any form of light.

- Heat, like light, is a natural enemy of wine, so keep your bottles away from any source of heat.

- Since wine likes a constant temperature, keep it out of rooms with temperatures that fluctuate more than 10 degrees up or down.

- Wine prefers a humid environment, not a dry one. Wine would be happily stored in a place that was 100 percent humidity.

- Don't keep your good wine standing on display. Wine isn't a decorative object or a conversation piece.

- Don't keep your white wine in the refrigerator for more than two to three weeks. Refrigerators are coolers, but they're also desiccators that will dry out the wine corks.

- Wine doesn't like to be shaken up, so keep it away from any vibrating mechanical system in your apartment, room in your house, or basement.

- Wine likes to lie on its side, so don't store bottles standing up.

- Red wines and white wines can be stored at the same temperature, which is ideally at 50–55 degrees. Keep the wines you'll have over the short term in a cool hall closet or other neutral kind of place.

TURNING BOTTLES: ANOTHER WINE MYTH

Needing to turn wine bottles in your wine rack or bins is a complete myth.

Somebody made up this "rule" ages ago and it's still pointless in terms of your care of the wine. One place where turning is a real issue is in the *making* of Champagne at the wineries where bottles are turned to force the sediment into the neck.

WHAT KIND OF STORAGE
IS RIGHT FOR YOU?

There's a wonderful scene in a wine cellar in the Alfred Hitchcock movie, *Notorious,* with Cary Grant and Ingrid Bergman. It is, in fact, in the cellar of a Nazi supporter and husband of the character played by Bergman. Cary Grant, the good guy, is surreptitiously given the key to the cellar door during a grand party at the house. It's a dark and shadowy cellar, and he accidentally knocks over a vintage bottle of Burgundy and to his surprise, it is filled with some black sand he believes is radioactive.

It's a fun movie. More to the point, the cellar was very evocative, romantic, and made you wonder what was in all the bottles.

Wine cellars can be a plot point, but you can have a *real* one built to your specifications and make it what you want it: beautiful, haunting, comforting or serene. It can be chic, cool, sexy, and fun. But what *is* a wine cellar?

Any space with four walls, temperature and humidity controls, proper insulation, and bins for the bottles can be called a wine cellar. A cellar doesn't have to be a room downstairs. It could a room in a one-story house. If you're serious about putting in a room where you can walk in and store fifty or more cases of wine, then you have to be set up properly. I would suggest that you hire a designer or contractor who has specific experience in building proper wine cellars. Ask for references. Ask to see pictures.

Everyone loves wine cellars. Some people get so excited that they're finally going to have a wine cellar that they decide to *entertain* there—to have dinners and parties at little tables set up among the bins. You don't want to entertain in a cellar.

It's a little too nippy in there. You don't want to sit around and have dinner in a room that's 55 degrees or possibly less, not to mention damp. You don't want to listen to music, dance, or socialize in such a room for more than a few minutes. You want to go there to retrieve a bottle and open it or bring some friends in for a few minutes of tasting pleasure.

The greatest cellars in the world are in England, Scotland, and Ireland because conditions there are cold *and* damp. English weather, it turns out, is as good for the wine as it is great for the skin.

That dampness is what you want, but a lot of cellar owners get upset because the labels on their bottles get what's known as "damp-stained" from the moisture. Often, when you buy expensive wines from a broker or dealer in Europe, they'll specify if a label is damp-stained. Wine auction catalogs also list damp-stained labels. Some people will pass up great wine because they want perfect labels, which is silly. This is just another version of drinking the label, not the wine.

I was in Illinois a few months ago to see new clients. Of course, they took me to their wine cellar. They had a little table and three fur jackets hanging on hooks. I thought it was funny when the wife of the couple told me, "These are my mother's old fur jackets. I don't wear them, so I keep them for women who find it's a bit cold for them down here." So we put on these little mink jackets, sat down, and tasted some superb Burgundy. It was a delightful experience.

There are many options open to you in the way of storage. If you have room for it, you can buy a *temperature-controlled wine cooler*. These units are available all over the country in stores that specialize in appliances or have large appliance departments where you can definitely find the small-size cooler, which is about the size of a 33-inch-tall refrigerator or freezer and about as wide. These units are not interchangeable with a small-size fridge. Prices start at about $250 and go up to about $4,000 for very large units.

Alternately, you can order a small- or large-capacity unit from *The Wine Enthusiast, International Wine Accessories,* or a number of other wine specialty catalogs.

You can convert a *whole closet* or use part of it. Don't hesitate to be resourceful and set up your wine collection here. Just be sure it's not next to a source of heat, or vulnerable to extreme cold. Keep it dark in there and stack your wine so every bottle is lying on its side. Try to keep the closet at a constant temperature, even if it tops out at 60–63 degrees. If you store wine in such a place that will not be there for more than a year, the wine will be okay and you're doing great.

However, you'll require a better system than a closet to store old, rare, and expensive wines. You'll need a serious, temperature- and humidity-controlled space.

Wine racks and bins are the most common means of stacking and storing bottles. I'm not partial to the words "wine rack," although I don't know what else to call the ubiquitous two-, three-, or four-tier units you can buy in shops like Hold Everything or the Pottery Barn. Thinking in professional oenological terms, wine doesn't go on shelves or on racks; it goes in *bins.* These bins are just the right size and depth and allow you to stack the bottles on top of each other.

One of my pet peeves is redwood racks in which you slide the bottles in and out. They may be a nice color, but the surface of the wood is all wrong—it scrapes and scratches the labels, minimizes the use of space, and you can't see what you have.

PROTECT YOUR WINE COLLECTION

If you can afford to amass a grand collection, you'll have to *limit access* to your total wine inventory. You don't want a cook (or the person cooking dinner at your house) poaching the pears in a $500 bottle of Sauternes when a $15 bottle would do nicely.

Such costly and wasteful mistakes are not that uncommon. I witnessed this very kind of mix-up in the dining room of a favorite client. I noticed a bottle of wine was missing from a case. When I questioned the cook, she unapologetically told me that she'd pulled a bottle to boil down for her beef stew. Nice work!

This cook believed her employers were rich enough to pour a whole bottle of $150 Tuscan wine into the pot. If there's a quarter of a cup or so left in an open bottle the next day, that's another story. Maybe then you can sacrifice it to the main course.

Although there's no reason to pour *great* wine into a pot that's going over a fire, you should follow the rule that you should be able to drink the wine you cook with. Above all, avoid the so-called salt-laden "cooking wines" you find in supermarkets. So even if you're rich enough, use good wine for the pot and save the great wine for the glass.

There can be greater wine-loss catastrophes than pouring one bottle of collectible wine in a stew pot. A friend of mine had to temporarily relocate to another city for at least six months while she worked on closing a deal for her company. An old friend of Karen's agreed to house-sit. Since she considered her friend totally trustworthy, she left her in charge. Karen returned to find the priceless cellar that she inherited from her father entirely gone—drunk up. Her good friend, the house sitter, kept the place fastidiously clean, but had a wonderful time raiding the wine cellar with no qualms.

Karen was devastated by the loss. It was more than the financial cost—it was a violation of her sentimental attachment to the collection, one that took her father time, effort, and loving care to amass. He'd bestowed it on Karen because he knew she'd take care of it.

Sometimes the loss is less momentous, but you still feel it. A client bought a really nice bottle of wine that she was saving to drink with her fiancé for his birthday. She went out of her way to find a bottle from his birth year. While she was away on vacation for a week at the beach, she let an out-of-town friend stay in her apartment. She drank the important vintage wine, but unlike the house sitter in the previous story, this woman tried to make her presumptuous poaching right: She replaced the bottle with the same brand, but *not* the same vintage year.

This is unfortunate, to say the least. She should have checked the label carefully and done the right thing, not any old thing.

You should no more be a snob than be disrespectful. Both extremes diminish your appreciation of wine.

So be aware that sometimes you have to protect your wine collection from the philistines, even if they are your friends. Know who is staying *on* your property and caring *for* your property. Be sure to establish house rules so your guests know what they can and cannot have access to.

Limiting access means you have to tell people not to take a bottle without your permission. If the collection is important and valuable enough to you, and the wine isn't easily replaceable, keep it under lock and key—whether it's from your teenagers, the people who repair your house or clean or cook for you, or any short-term or long-term guests.

Limiting access sounds obvious, but it's a rule some people don't think about or hesitate to bring up. It's important to remember in the matter of collecting wine.

COLLECTING LABELS AND EMPTY WINE BOTTLES

I often keep empty wine bottles, if only to continue admiring the labels, which can be little works of decorative art. Other times, I want to keep the empty bottle to remember whom I was with when I shared that specific wine. Sometimes, I jot down the date I had the wine, with whom, and maybe a little comment right on the side of a label.

This makes empty bottles a very personal kind of collectible. If there's an important occasion, open an important bottle of wine and keep it on display, with the details on the label. When you look back on it, it brings back fantastic memories.

Right now in my kitchen, I have an empty bottle of a '55 Château Latour, dated and drunk on April 29, 1997. I was with my friend Fritz who wrote on it in his bold script, "Judy's taste knows no bounds. It encompasses the classic, the exotic, the surprising, but never the merely good." He was definitely inspired after sharing this bottle with me. Yet another that means a lot to me was inscribed by a friend who wrote on the label, "What a wine. Bottled decadence."

Keep the empty bottles, or if you like, soak the labels off (or get a new gadget that removes labels and laminates them) and keep them in a scrapbook of some sort.

WINE AS AN INVESTMENT

The primary motivation in buying wine is *not* as a financial instrument, but for the magic and pleasure in the wine itself. Anyone I've ever met who tried to invest in wine for financial gain alone has failed abysmally. It's the wrong attitude and the wrong karma for wine.

I've seen people who've approached "wine futures" with greed in mind, thinking certain wines are fast turnovers for profits. The quick-fix mentality can doom you in this business. So can hubris. I got a call from Wendy, a woman who made a lot of money in the bond market, her area of expertise on Wall Street. She told me that she had $500,000 to invest in wine. She was calling me for advice on what to buy.

I began asking her a few questions about where she was going to house the wine for the long run, when she interrupted me. "I don't really need you after you tell me what to buy. I've got it all set up. I'm going to hold on to the wine for five years, then I'm going to sell it and make twenty-five to thirty percent on my money." She caught her breath and continued, ". . . and I guess I'll have to call you again in five years because then I need to know where to sell it."

I said, "Wendy, you don't need me at all. But you've given me a good idea. I think I'm going to start my own bond fund. So, good luck," I told her. "If you think that investing in wine works according to your system, you are sorely mistaken!"

Wendy's five-year-turnover gambit has little to do with the very complex wine investment business. I'd never tell a client, "Give this five years to get your money back." In five years' time we might be in a recession and you *wouldn't* sell your wine just yet. There's no formula that works across the board where X amount of dollars is guaranteed to yield XX amount in Y number of years. Rather—and this is what I stress when people ask me about investing in wine—it is a long-term *asset-managed strategy.*

This is really important for you to heed: When you invest in wine, you are developing an investment portfolio which has to be managed and scrutinized. This means the person in charge of the management is doing everything from following global market trends to currency fluctuations to trends in buying and selling wine on a worldwide basis.

You cannot play a buy-hold-sell game based on anyone else's history with investing in wine. It doesn't matter that Wendy knew someone who did the five- year turnover and made some money on it. The market changes. Buyers and sellers change. The wine that's available changes. Unless you're an expert in the international wine market, you really need advice from an expert in the business.

WINE, THE COMMODITY

Now that I've given you my thoughts on the heart of the matter, let's turn to the brains—thinking and planning wisely. As an investment, wine can be auctioned, traded, or bought for resale, depending on the vintage and producer. If you're thinking of wine in terms of futures, you need to know how to protect your investment and help insure that the wine you buy now is resalable later.

There's really one critical question you have to ask yourself about investing in wine after you figure out if you want to collect wine for your own long-term enjoyment, as a legacy for

THE MYTH OF THE QUICK FIX

There's no quick fix for anything worthwhile in life, including the belief that good vintage wine can make you your fortune. Buying for the future is like cultivating a relationship with another human being—and the difference between marrying solely for money or for looks. Without the soul, it's no marriage. With wine, don't invest in it entirely because of the label.

Then again, you might be immediately attracted to a person you want to know or even love, but it takes time to understand that person and cultivate and develop a relationship with him or her. And, of course, there's no guarantee that the relationship will work. It's the same thing with wine. You have to give it time.

If you're looking for a quick fix in something worthwhile, enjoy the quick fix now and buy a good bottle of Champagne. Open it. Invest in your drinking pleasure with people whose company you like.

your children (or someone else), or if you want to collect as a financial investment: Who will oversee your minicollection, or if you go big, a full cellar?

If you buy a thoroughbred, you don't leave it in the care of a guy who's scared of horses. The same is true for wine collecting. It means having a skillful, loving professional (a consultant hired specifically for the job) who can wisely administer proper wine cellar management, collection, and resale. Don't put an amateur in charge of one of your most prized investments.

There's mystique in this commodity.

There's nothing new about investing in wine for profit, which is a very, very old practice. I run a business that specializes in putting together and managing high-end wine collections both for pleasure and, in the case of certain clients, for financial investment. I've been working at it for twenty years, joining a long line of tradition in the business. You have to have the heart for it.

How do you find wine to invest in?

Other than stocks and bonds, some serious investors also finance something called "alternative investments," one of which is wine. This could comprise about five percent of their portfolios. This is where you reach into the really sophisticated, rarified world of big money. If you're talking about investing for financial gain, you have to be in the big leagues. Be prepared to start out with at least one hundred thousand dollars to invest. Otherwise, it's like buying three shares of stock.

Europeans have invested in wines going back generations—that is, back hundreds of years. Buying in quantity for the future was not originally about speculation and a fast turnover, but long-term investment. This philosophy is still the backbone of the trade.

The idea is to buy the best wines as young as possible and to buy more than you can drink, say, ten cases just released from the château or the wine maker. Then you lay it down. Eventually, when it's ready to drink in eight or ten or fifteen years, and usually no sooner than eight years, you can always sell at least nine of the ten cases you've bought. At this point, if you've done it correctly, prices will have risen. I always recommend that you keep either a bottle or case of the wine for yourself, and drink it essentially for free, because of the profit you've made from the sale.

The Numbers Crunch

People always ask me what the return on investment is for wine. This is not unlike asking a stock broker to estimate exactly how much your stock portfolio will rise by next year. I can't give you an exact percentage, but I can tell you this: Fine investment-grade wines have always been equal to or outperformed financial indices.

If you're in the business, you must track the prices of investment-grade wines. Historically, this is about the best wines bought at the best price and bought at the right time.

What I do for clients is kind of simple and yet it's not so simple. Basically, I know eight things: *what to buy, when to buy it, where to buy it,* and *how much to pay.* When I'm managing those wines as an investment on behalf of a client, I will also know: *what to sell, when to sell it, where to sell it in the world,* and *for how much.* This is the kind of expertise anyone should have who's running any kind of portfolio—stocks, art, or any commodity with an investment base to it.

The thing about wine is, unlike stocks, there's a finite amount of it. IBM can issue more shares and split its stock two for one, but you can only make four thousand cases of Petrus. That's it for that wine, or for whatever other wine sold for investment.

However, and this is a big "however," I wouldn't tell anyone to buy Petrus, for example, as a foolproof investment. There's a lot more to it than that. Before buying a single bottle of it, I'd need to know its *provenance,* just as I would a painting or a piece of antique furniture. In other words, where has this wine been? Has it traded hands? Has it been badly or carefully stored? Has it been badly or carefully shipped? Did the owner buy it at auction and pay too much, then decide to sell it quickly? Did someone "forget" to tell me that the guy kept the Petrus dockside in Hong Kong for four years and then sent it back for resale?

In a way, that answers another question people ask me

about *which* wine to invest in. My answer is: First, buy the best wine from the top producers and be sure it's in top condition. Second, realize that there's a minimum investment and, third, you need the expertise.

An expert in wines usually doesn't live in your neighborhood. Some experts can be found at auction houses, but you should really do your own research. But there *are* also independent experts. There aren't that many of us in the world, but we can be found and hired to advise you on your wine investment. Then again, you can do your homework and make wine your passion and pursue this area of the market.

Invest in Your Own Drinking Future

Your wine may stand up historically and become a really interesting investment, but there are no guarantees that you'll make the profit you'd hoped. The soundest investment is in your own drinking pleasure. You should always be prepared to liquidate your investment by drinking it.

WINE ACCESSORIES AND ANTIQUES

This is a real hands-on kind of adjunct to collecting wine that's a lot more inclusive and a lot of fun. Whether you're in the market for gorgeous crystal glasses from the Georgian period in England or new Champagne flutes from the Pottery Barn, you'll get a lot of gratification in what you can find in the area of wine collectibles.

I'm a fan of flea markets and outdoor antique fairs where I've picked up, for example, wonderful silver-plated coasters that are just the right size to hold a bottle of wine on the table. Many people find clear glass decanters of every age and size in thrift stores and at local tag sales.

I can't resist a fantastic decanter, even if the stopper is chipped or missing. You get a great deal on the not-so-perfect ones. I find old decanters quite beautiful. Decanters of any age make fantastic collectibles and always flatter wine, red or white. Be sure it's a wine decanter, not a square-sided one which is really for hard liquor, like bourbon. Wine decanters have a rounded shape. There are a million different designs and, it seems, no two the same. When you buy one, just make sure it has enough capacity in it for one bottle of wine.

It's always fun to decant your bottle of wine so you get to admire the color, even white wine, in clear glass. Remember: Wine is usually bottled in green or yellow glass to protect it from the light.

You can easily begin a wine-glass collection, and since mix-and-match is the rule, you don't have to worry about getting a perfect service for twelve. Glasses don't have to be Irish crystal or French Lalique antiques, unless these are to your liking. Glasses don't have to be expensive—they just have to be the right shape for the wine. Avoid those wide-mouth V-shaped glasses for wine. They're great looking, but you can't swirl your wine in them or capture the bouquet.

Other than haunting flea markets or antique shops for wine collectibles, you can check catalogs, such as *The Wine Enthusiast,* and get anything you want from elegant to cutesy. It's up to you. But you will need a few essential wine accessories.

In terms of collectibles, you can also look for vintage advertising posters for wines and spirits going back to the 1920s. There are picnic baskets fitted out with sections for the bottle of wine, the glasses, and no doubt, the cheese and the bread.

It's a great area to investigate, so have fun doing it!

A FINAL NOTE

I mentioned a client earlier in chapter 6 on occasions, who has a huge party every year around Christmastime—a formal sit-down dinner for 190 people. The first year that I did the wine for this couple, I said I thought it would be fun to use jeroboams and imperials—the biggest bottles—and decant the wine as the guests walked in to dinner.

They agreed. We had forty decanters set up where I poured wine with a couple of assistants. The empty bottles were piled up at the end of this long table in a big jumble. Everyone kept coming up to the table to watch. They loved seeing the visual aspect of decanting, which can be exciting.

So don't hide the bottles, the openers, the coasters, the decanting equipment, or anything else involving the wine experience. Old or new, bring it all out to the table, even if you have a galley kitchen and live in a studio apartment. The pleasure of wine goes beyond the ceremony of lifting your glass to toast—it's bringing everything about wine together in one place.

IN CONCLUSION . . .

MAKE WINE PART OF YOUR LIFE

The simple truth is that if you can find five or six wines you really like, can afford, and have ready access to in your home, you're way ahead. You need not take a course in wine to enjoy its variety and bounty—you're already living it if you've got a good glass of wine in your hand for dinner. Don't concern yourself about what to say about the gift of the grape: Drinking wine will always be about pleasure first.

BIBLIOGRAPHY AND
RESOURCE DIRECTORY

❖

I've put together a short list of references, a wine-country tour, and other sources for you to learn more about wine.

An Interesting Wine Tour
Lidia's Esperienze Italiane
(Italian food, wine, and culture)
Custom designed for groups of 4 to 60
1-800-480-2426

This tour was created by world-famous chef and restaurateur, Lidia Bastianich, owner of Felidia and two other restaurants in New York and host of her own cooking show on PBS stations. It's great fun and wonderfully organized.

Books and Sources: The Essential Wine Reference Library

Hugh Johnson's World Atlas of Wine by Hugh Johnson
How to Taste by Jancis Robinson
Passions, The Wines and Travels of Thomas Jefferson by
    James M. Gabler
The Oxford Companion to Wine by Jancis Robinson
The Great Vintage Wine Book by Michael Broadbent
Bordeaux by Robert M. Parker, Jr.
Burgundy by Robert M. Parker, Jr.
Burton Anderson's Best Italian Wines by Burton Anderson
Cooking with Wine by Anne Willan
An Omelette and a Glass of Wine by Elizabeth David

Newsstand or Subscription Magazines

Decanter
www.Decanter.com

The Wine Spectator
www.WineSpectator.com

Robert M. Parker, Jr.'s The Wine Advocate
P.O. Box 311
Monkton, MD 21111
410-329-6477

Wine Bridal Registry

Sherry-Lehmann Wines and Spirits
679 Madison Avenue
New York, NY 10021
212-838-7500
www.sherry-lehmann.com

Wine Glasses

The Wine Enthusiast

(For Riedel brand and other wine glasses, decanters, and
home wine cellar needs)

1-800-356-8466

www.wineenthusiast.com

WINE GADGETS AND WOMEN

I recently saw a segment pitching Christmas holiday gifts on a
morning network talk show, this one featuring a wine accessories
kit. It consisted of a corkscrew, a cork, etc., and was presented as
"In the Guy's Category." I object! There are women who buy such
sets for themselves and for other women. Ignore this kind of
exclusionary sales talk. Wine is for everyone.

INDEX

A
Aaron, Michael, 86–87
Accessories, 193–94
Acidity, 16, 121
Acquiring a taste, 21
Aftertaste, 21
Alcohol, 22, 63, 72
Alcoholic content, 16, 29–30
Alcoholic drinks, 64–65
Alsace, 34–35, 141, 153
    Gewürztraminer, 121
    Pinot Gris, 113
    Riesling, 179
Alto Adige (Südtirol), 44, 45
America, 50, 51–53
American Wine Alliance for Research
    and Education, (AWARE), 65
Ansonica (grape), 46
Antioxidants, 65, 66, 75, 80
Argentina, 56
Aroma(s), 14, 167
    Bordeaux wines, 38–39

Chardonnay, 27
    releasing, 110
    Riesling, 49
    Riojas, 47
    swirling to get, 116
    white wine, 31
Aroma wheels, 18
Asset-managed strategy, 189
Australia, 17, 53–55, 151
    Chardonnay, 54, 134

B
Balance, 15–16
Barbaresco, 46
Barbera (grape), 43, 56
Barbera (wine), 119–20
Barolo, 1, 44, 46
Beardsall Rule-of-Thumb Restaurant
    Price Guide, 171
Beaujolais (region), 26, 42
Beaujolais (wine), 15, 29, 94, 154
    for occasions, 126, 133

INDEX

Beauty, wine and, 79–81
Bellavista, 47
Blanc de Blancs, 36
Blanquette de Limoux, 37
Body, 22
Bollinger, 37, 179
Bonterra, 74
Bordeaux (region), 26, 31–32,
    52–53, 65, 149
    vineyards of, 69
Bordeaux (wine), 60, 122, 131, 132
    aging, 39
    Grand Crus, 69
    as health tonic, 73–74
    red, 29, 37–39, 67
    for starter cellar, 179
    therapeutic virtues of, 77–78
    white, 141
Bordeaux varietal(s), 56
Borsao Rioja, 97
Bottles, 34
    collecting, 187
    color of, 16, 111, 194
    feeling, 166
Bottles of wine
    checking level of wine in, 165
    lying on sides, 107–08, 181, 184
    in restaurant, 164–68
    sending back, 155–56, 164–65
    uncorked, 164–65
Bourgogne Blanc, 33, 97, 132, 154
Bourgogne Rouge, 150
Bourgueil, 112
Brunello di Montalcino, 46
Burgundies, 10, 143
    red, 26, 37–38, 40–42, 149–50
    white, 26, 33, 89, 132, 170–71
Burgundy (region), 26, 27, 32–33, 163

C
Cabernet, 132
    Napa Valley, 134
Cabernet Franc (grape), 33, 38
Cabernet Sauvignon (grape), 38,
    52, 53
    in Australian wines, 54
    Chile, 56
    France, 46

South America, 56
Cabernet Sauvignon (wine), 18, 55,
    134
Cabernet Sauvignon-based wine, 122
California, xii, 27
    Pinot Noir, 133
    wine industry, 26, 50, 51, 52–53
    wines, 52–53, 120
Cancer-fighting properties of wine,
    71, 74
Care of wine(s), 101–16
    do's and don'ts (list), 180–81
    short-term, 103–08
Casa Lapostelle Chardonnay, 97
Case(s) of wine, 100, 174, 178
Catechin, 65
Caterers, 127–28, 130
Chablis, 27, 119
Chadderdon, Robert, 98
Champagne (region), 3, 26, 35–36,
    37, 149
Champagne (wine), 3, 27, 29, 30,
    35–37, 80, 90, 119, 140, 190
    all-purpose wine, 132, 178
    as dessert wine, 154–55
    first, 36
    with food, 123
    glasses for, 36, 115, 193
    making of, 181
    for occasions, 126, 130, 135
    rosé, 134
    for starter cellar, 179
    tasting samples for customers,
        85–86
    therapeutic virtues of, 77, 79–80
Champagne flutes, 36, 193
Champagne houses, 36, 37, 112
Character (wine), 4, 5, 31
Chardonnay (grape), 26, 27, 32, 34,
    46, 53, 156–57
    for Champagne, 36
    Chile, 56
    white wines from Burgundy, 33
Chardonnays, 21, 23
    Australian, 54, 134
    California, 54
    Casa Lapostelle Chardonnay, 97
    Chilean, 57

Edna Valley Chardonnay, 97
grape/region dilemma, 26
    Italy, 44
    New Zealand, 55
    Trevor Jones, 142
    for wine occasions, 134
Château Lafite, 32
Château Latour, 9, 12, 187
Château Margaux, 12, 25–26
Château Mouton, 32
Château Smith-Haut-Lafitte, 79
Châteauneuf-du-Pape, 40, 132
Châteaux (wine estates), 32
Chianti (region), 26
Chianti (wine), 9, 26, 90, 122
    grape blends in, 44
    Italy, 45
Chile, 56, 144
Chilled wines, 36, 99–100
Cholesterol, 66, 67, 71, 77
Christmas, 118, 124–25, 126, 132,
    195
Cinnamasta, x
Clerks (wine shop), 85, 93, 94, 99
    recommendations by, 94–95
Climate, 3, 39, 44, 54, 56
Collectibles, 193–94
Collecting wine/wine collection,
    173–95
    how much to buy now, 174
    limiting access to, 185, 186–87
    protecting, 185–87
    reasons for starting, 175
    starting, 174–81
    starting: ground rules, 178
Color of wine, 16–18, 111, 113–14,
    166, 194
    in matching food to wine, 120
Commodity, wine as, 189–91
Common cold, wine and, 70
Cooking wines, 185
Cork
    checking, 166
    pieces of, in wine, 167
    pulling, 108
    shrunk, 107, 108
    sound of, 108–09
Cork sniffing, myth of, 15, 23

Corkscrew, 108, 167
Corton-Charlemagne, 7–8
Côtes-du-Rhône, 40, 132, 154
Côtes-du-Rhône "Reserve," 97
Country
    wine list organized by, 148–49
    wines organized by, 89
Cristal Champagne, 35
Critics and reviewers, language used
    by, 11–12, 13
Crôzes-Hermitage, 143, 160
Cru Beaujolais, 42
Cru bourgeois, 32
Crus/grands crus, 32, 33, 42
    Bordeaux, 69

D
Decanters, 16, 110, 111
    collecting, 194
Decanting, 101, 109, 110–11,
    195
Derain, Monsieur, 163–64
Dessert wines, 122, 124, 154–55
Diet, 61, 68, 72
Digestion, wine aids, 66, 68
Dinner(s), 68, 134
Display, 106–07, 181
Dom Perignon Champagne, 36
Domaine Leflaive, 33
Domaine Weinbach (Collette Faller
    et Ses Filles), 34–35
Dressner, Louis, 98
Drinking the label, 6–7, 183
Drinking wine
    every day, 60, 62, 75, 76, 118
    versus not drinking wine,
    75–77
Dry wine, 48, 49, 66

E
Easter, 126, 132
Edna Valley Chardonnay, 97
Empson, Neil, 98
Entre-deux-Mers, 78
EPIDOS, 73
Erbacher Marcobrunn, 117
European Institute of Wine Health
    Society, 65

INDEX

European wine producers
   rules for labeling, 26–27

F
Fading, 17
Feelings evoked by wines, 2, 8–9,
   10, 11
Fetzer Vineyards, 74
Feudi di San Gregorio, 45–46
Fiano di Avellino grape, 171
Finish, 21
Fish, wines to accompany, 49, 117,
   120, 121, 122, 152
Flavor(s), 13, 20, 31
   Bordeaux wines, 38–39
   categories of, on wine list, 148
   Gamay grape, 42
   in matching wine to food, 120
   wines from Burgundy, 32
   wines organized by, 89–90
Fleurie, 42, 154
Food, matching wine to, 49, 118,
   119–20, 121–24, 131–32,
   134, 152–53, 154
   breaking rules, 123–24
   guidelines, 120–24
   in restaurants, 138–39
Fragrance, checking, 166
France, 151
   Chardonnay grape, 27
   Medoc Marathon, 68–70
   red wines, 37–42
   white wines, 31–37
   wines from, on wine list, 148,
   149
Franciacorta region, 47
French Paradox, 61–62, 67
Friuli, 46
Future, laying down wine for, 173,
   176–77, 191
Futures (wine), 188, 189

G
Gamay (grape), 26, 42
Garnet Wines, 85–86, 87–89
Germany, 30–31, 34, 48–50
Gevrey-Chambertin, 150
Gewürztraminer, 4, 49

Alsace, 121
Glasses, 112–14
   clear, rounded, with stem, 16,
   114
   collecting, 193, 194
   colored, 112–14
   filling one-third full, 110, 116,
   167
   fluted, for Champagne, 36, 193
   holding by stem, 115–16
   refilling, 167–68
   shapes and sizes, 115, 116
   sniffing, 23
   "tasting," 116
   wine breathes in, 109–10
Goldwater Estate, Dog Point
   Vineyard, 55
   Sauvignon Blanc, 97
Grape extracts, 80
Grape/region dilemma, 25–28
Grape seeds, 79–80
Grape skins, 66, 67, 72, 79, 80
Grape type, wines organized by, 90
Grape varietals
   Burgundy, 32
   Italy, 45–46
   on wine list, 148
Grapes, 2, 7
   from Bordeaux, 31–32, 38
   from Champagne region of France,
   3, 37
   fermented, 29
   in French red wine, 39–40
   in French white wine, 33
   Italy, 43–44
   quality of, 54
   for Riesling, 30–31
   South America, 56
   weather affecting, 28
   see also Merlot grape; Nebbiolo
   grape; Sauvignon Blanc grape;
   Syrah grape
Grenache (grape), 39, 40

H
Haut-Brion, 137–38
Health, wine and, 59–81
   through history, 62–64

Health-giving properties of wine,
    60–61, 63–64, 66, 69, 71,
    72, 74–75, 76, 77, 179
Health Through the Grape, 79
Heart disease/attack, 61, 65, 66, 67,
    72, 76, 77
Heart protection by wine, 71–72
Heat, protecting wine from, 103–04,
    179, 180, 184
Hermitage, 132
High-density lipoproteins (HDL), 71
Hippocrates, 62
House wine(s), 156–57, 160
Hugel (producer), 35
Humidity, 105–06, 107, 179, 181,
    184

I
Importer's name on label, 97–98, 165
Instant gratification, 175–78
Intention of wine, 1, 2
International Wine Accessories, 184
Investment, wine as, 188–91
    return on investment, 191–93
    in your own drinking future, 193
Italian restaurants, 149
Italian wines, 149
    red, 43, 45
    for starter cellar, 179
    white, 43, 44–47
Italy, 42–44, 151
    food/wine match in, 119–20
    regions, 43–44, 46

J
Judy Beardsall General Rule of Party
    Wine Buying, 130
Judy Beardsall's Recommended
    Wines for $10–15, 97
Judy Beardsall's Sample Starter Cellar,
    179

K
Kacher, Robert, 98

L
Label(s), 4, 44–45
    alcohol percentage on, 29

checking, 165
collecting, 187
damp-stained, 183
drinking, 6–7, 183
information on, 97–98
Labeling, 26–27, 48–49, 53
Languedoc, 33–34, 40, 89, 97
    red wine, 37, 97
Lazio, 46
Leaky capsule, checking for, 165
Leftover wine, 113
"Legs," 22
Leroy, 33
Light
    protecting wine from, 16, 103,
        179, 180, 194
Locascio, Leonardo, 98
Loire Valley, 33–34, 37, 55, 93, 112,
    149, 154
Lombardy, 46
Long Island, xii, 93
Longevity, wine and, 73–74
Low-density lipoproteins (LDL), 71
Lower Hunter Valley (Australia), 54
Lynch, Kermit, 98
Lyon, 41–42

M
Mâcon-Villages, 27, 148, 154
Madeira, 119
Main course, wines with, 154
Malbec, 56
Manzanilla, 48
Margaux region (Bordeaux), 25–26
Mas de Gourgonnier, 97
Mass-market wines, 5, 89
Maturity, color and, 17, 18
Meals, wine with, 43, 45–46, 77
Meat, red wine with, 120, 121, 122
Medicinal values of wine, 62–64
Mediterranean cultures, 75
Medoc (region), 78
Medoc Marathon, 68–70
Memorial Day, 132
Mendocino (county), 51
Merlot grape, 26, 38, 46, 54, 156–57
Merlots, 143
Misobibists, xii

Mission Haut-Brion, La, 101–02
Moderation, 62, 69, 73, 75, 76, 77, 81
Moët et Chandon, 140
Montefalco Rosso, 97
Montrachet Grand Cru, 169
Morgon, 154
Moulin-à-Vent, 42
"Mouth feel," 22–23
Muscat de Baumes-de-Venise, 124, 133
Myth(s), xi, 5
 cork sniffing, 15
 foods matching wines, 121–22
 German wines, 48
 quick fix, 190
 red wine with cheese, 123
 removing cork to let wine breathe,
  109–10
 swirling wines, 116
 turning bottles, 181
 winespeak, 11
 women and wine list, 144

N
Napa (county), 51
Napa Valley, 50, 80
 Cabernet, 134
 Château Montelena, 164–65
Nebbiolo grape, 10, 43, 44, 46, 90,
  120, 148
New Year's, 128, 132
New Zealand, 55, 151, 154
Nutritional benefits of wine, 65–68

O
Occasions
 budget, 129–30
 location, 127–28
 how many bottles to order, 130
 number of people, 128
 planned around wine, 133–35
 planning for, 126
 quality of wine for, 130–31
 season, 128–29
 steps in preparing for, 124–31
 wine for, 117–35
Oloroso, 48
Opening wine, 108–10
Ordonez, Jorge, 98

Organic wineries, 74
Osteoporosis, 66, 73, 74
Ostertag (producer), 141

P
Palacios (producer), 144
Passion of wine, x, 1, 2, 5
Passion
 for wine, ix, 18
 in wine production, 57
Penedes, 48
Petrus, 107–08, 192
Phenolic components, 71
Philosophies of wine, 1–2, 52–53
Phylloxera, 51
Piedmont, 10, 44, 46, 120, 179
 grape from, 148
 reds from, 133
Pinot Bianco, 23, 44–45
Pinot Blanc, 97, 133, 141, 153
Pinot Grigio, 44, 45, 142
Pinot Gris, 44, 153
 Alsace, 113
Pinot Noir (grape), 32, 40, 41, 52, 90
 for Champagne, 36
 South America, 56
Pinot Noir (wine), 3, 123, 154
 California, 133
Pol-Roger, Christian, 86
Pol-Roger, 37, 86, 179
Polyphenols, 65, 71, 75, 79–80
Port, 123, 132, 155
Potassium, 67–68
Pouilly-Fumé, 33–34
Pouilly-Fuissé, 27, 34, 38
Presentation, 164–65
Prices, 32, 96, 97
 restaurants, 138, 169–71
 restaurants: formula for, 170–71
Priorato (region), 48, 144
Producer(s), 57, 149, 150, 189
 small, 45, 89, 99
Professionals
 to administer wine collection, 190
 terminology used by, 10–11
Prohibition, 50, 51–52, 54, 64, 92
Prosecco, 126
Provenance, 192

Provence, 149
Puligny-Montrachet, 27, 150, 164

Q
Quality control, 6
Quercetin, 70
Quick fix, myth of, 190

R
Rauenthaler Rothenberg Riesling
    Spatlese, 117
Rausan-Segla, 25–26
Recommendations, 93, 94–95
    author's, 35, 97, 140–44, 153, 154
    clerks, 94–95
    sommelier, 127, 137–38, 160–61
Red wines, 30, 67, 150–51
    Australia, 53–54
    Burgundy, 32
    cancer-fighting properties of, 71
    color variations, 17–18
    from crus in Bordeaux, 32
    flavors, 13
    France, 37–42
    health benefits of, 65, 71, 72, 74, 78
    Italy, 43, 45
    Languedoc, 97
    Loire Valley, 112
    matching to food, 120, 121, 122
    New Zealand, 55
    nutritional benefits of, 66
    for occasions, 132, 133
    restaurant meals, 154
    South America, 56
    Spain, 48
    for starter cellar, 179
    temperature, 106, 181
Ridge Zinfandel, 142
Refrigeration, 106, 181
Region(s), 3–4, 31–42
    finding wines by, 93
    wine list organized by, 149
    see also Grape/region dilemma
Remelluri (producer), 179
Resource directory, 197–99
Restaurants, 137–71
    by-the-glass pour, 154, 156, 157
    pricing wine, 169–71

receiving wine ordered, 164–68
Resveritrol, 66, 67
Rhône Valley, 37, 39–40, 132
Ribero del Duero, 48
Riesling (grape), 26, 49
Rieslings, 30–31, 49–50, 133, 179
Rioja (region), 47, 48
Riojas, 47, 154, 174, 179
Rosé, 133, 134
Rothschild, Baron Philippe de, 52

S
Saint-Amour, 42
Saint-Aubin, 132, 163–64
St. Emilion region, 78
St. Véran, 132
Sancerre, 33–34, 148, 154
Sangiovese (grape), 26, 43, 44, 46
Sassacaia, 46
Saumur Champigny, 133
Sauternes, 78, 122, 124, 179, 185
Sauvignon Blanc (wine), 21–22, 55,
    133
    Italy, 44
    New Zealand, 55, 154, 156
Sauvignon Blanc grape, 21–22, 33,
    34, 152
Screwpull, 108
Searle, Ronald, 11–12
Seasonal entertaining, 131–33
Sediment, 111
Sense memory training, 19
Sensory associations, 9, 12–13, 14, 16
Sensory components of wine, 16–23
Sherry, 47–48, 132, 134
Sherry-Lehmann Wine and Spirits,
    ix, 86–88
Shiraz, 53–54, 132
Sicily, 46, 120, 142, 179
Skurnik, Michael, 98
Smell of wine, 18–19
Soil character, 3, 39
Solaia, 46
Sommelier, 157–62, 165, 168
    ordering without, 162
    recommendations, 127, 137–38,
        160–62
    stories from, 163–64

Sonoma (county), 51
Sonoma-Cutrer, 141
Sound of wine, 23
Sources de Caudalie, 79–80
South America, 56–57
Spain, 47–48, 144
Spargelwein, 152
Sparkling wines, 35, 37, 90
    for occasions, 126, 130
Spoilage, 155–56, 166
Standards (wine), 5–8
Storage, 100, 166, 182–84
Stress reduction, 68, 69–70
Structure, 38, 43
Style of wine, 1, 2, 5, 14–16
    California wines, 53
    Champagne, 37
    Riesling, 49
    Sauvignon Blanc, 55
SuperTuscans, 46
Sweet wines, 119, 124, 133
    Germany, 48, 49–50
    for starter cellar, 179
Swirling the wine, 116
Syrah (wine), 54, 91
Syrah grape, 39–40, 46, 53, 54

T
Tannin (tannic acid), 20, 65, 78, 111,
    121
Taste, 14, 20–22, 49
    Gamay grape, 42
    in matching food to wine, 120
    smell and, 19
    white wine, 31
Tastevin, 158–59
Tasting, 166–67
"Tasting" glasses, 111
Temperature, 104, 106, 113, 166,
    181, 184
    wine when served, 111–12
Temperature-controlled wine cooler,
    183–84
Tenuta di Trinoro, 162
Terroir, 3, 4, 32, 57
    Bordeaux, 31–32
    Burgundy, 33
    California, 52, 53

    Champagne, 36
    French red wines, 39, 40
    South America, 56
Testamatta, 46
Texture, 23
Thallasotherapy, 59–61, 68
Thanksgiving, 126, 133
Therapeutic Virtues of Champagne,
    The, 78–79
Therapeutic virtues of wine, 77–79
Tokay Pinot Gris, 133
Trentino-Alto Adige, 46
Trevor Jones (producer), 142
Trimbach (producer), 35
Turning bottles, myth of, 181
Tuscany, 46, 93, 133, 179

U
United States Pharmacopeia National
    Formulary, 63

V
Vac-u-vin, 113
Valentine's Day, 117–18, 132
Vega Sicilia, 48
Veratrole, 65
Vermentino (grape), 46
Veuve Cliquot, 145
Vibrations, 106, 181
Vineyards, 5
    Alsace, 34–35
    America, xi-xii
    Burgundy, 33
    California, 51, 52
    South America, 56
Vinotherapy, 79–80
Vintage, 28–29, 189
    Champagne, 37
    checking, 165
    Italian white wines, 46
    on wine list, 149, 150
    wines from Burgundy, 33
Vitiano, 97
Vouvray, 37, 133, 141

W
Waiters, 151, 156, 158, 165, 168
Weight (wine), 29, 120

Weygandt, Peter, 98
White wines, 4, 27, 30–31, 65, 67
    color variations, 17, 114
    flavors, 13
    France, 31–37
    Germany, 48
    health benefits of, 74–75, 78
    Italy, 43, 44–47
    matching to food, 120, 121, 122,
        152
    New Zealand, 55
    nutritional benefits of, 66
    for occasions, 132, 133
    with restaurant meals, 152, 153,
        154
    South America, 56–57
    for starter cellar, 179
    temperature, 106, 181
Wine
    breathing, 108, 109–10, 111,
        167
    as commodity, 189–91
    daily intake, 60, 62, 75, 76, 118
    essence of, 57
    finding, 93
    healthy attitude toward, 81
    how displayed in store, 98–99
    how much to buy, 100, 155
    investment-grade, 192
    is good for you, 60, 61, 75
    making part of life, xii, 195
    masculine/feminine, 12
    natural chemistry of, 29
    opening up, 110
    organized in store, 99
    shopping with list, 93–94
    transporting, 102
Wine basics, 29–30
Wine business, ix-x, 86–87, 190–91
    German, 48–49
    standards, 5–8
    women and, 145
Wine cellars, 104, 105, 106, 107,
        131, 158, 177, 182–84
    minicellar, 178–81
    restaurants, 146–47, 169
    short-, medium-, long-term, 178
Wine culture, xi

Wine Enthusiast, The, 184, 194
Wine experience, 2, 92, 195
    food in, 121
    in restaurant, 161
    sommelier in, 158
    wine glasses in, 114
Wine industry
    in America, 52, 64
    in California, 26, 50, 51, 52–53
Wine language/winespeak, 8–14,
        20, 49
Wine list(s), 97, 137, 138, 139–44
    categories on, 148–51
    expensive, 149–51
    information on, 147
    organization of, 145–51
    selecting from, 151–54
    size of, 147–48
    who gets, xi, 144–46
Wine makers
    Australia, 54–55
    Burgundy, 32
    Italy, 45–46
    small, 5, 28
    women, 145
Wine making, 4
    America, 52–53
    Australia, 53–55
    human element in, 27–28
    international style of, 4–5
    soil and climate in, 39
    South America, 56
Wine-pairing guidelines, 120–24,
        131–32
Wine racks/bins, 184
Wine sense, 1–23
Wine shops, 83–100, 130
    checking conditions in, 98–99
    establishing relationship with,
        88
    great, 96
    how set up, 87–92
    negotiating, 92–93
    positive thinking, 84–85
    types of, 85–87
Wine specialty catalogs, 184, 194
Wine-Tasters' Logic (Simon), 12
Wine types, wines organized by, 90

INDEX

Women
  and wine, xi, 66, 73
  and wine business, 145
  and wine list, 144–46

X
X factors, 3, 27
  see also *Terroir*

Z
Zind-Humbrecht (producer), 35
Zinfandel, 53, 122, 132
  Ridge Zinfandel, 142